Groups at Work

Strategies and Structures
for Professional Learning

by
Laura Lipton and Bruce Wellman

Page layout, cover design and illustrations
by Michael Buckley

MiraVia®
The Road To Learning
www.miravia.com

Groups at Work

Strategies and Structures
for Professional Learning

by

Laura Lipton and Bruce Wellman

Copyright © 2011 by MiraVia, LLC

10 9 8 7 6 5
Fourth printing, April 2016
Printed in the United States of America
ISBN 978-0-9665022-7-5 Softcover
Library of Congress Control Number: 2010911244

MiraVia, LLC
236 Lucy's Lane Charlotte, VT 05445
www.miravia.com

Dedication

This book is dedicated
to the groups and group leaders
that have let us experiment
and refine our work
in their world.

Acknowledgements

This work has been enhanced by countless conversations with colleagues who have shared their dilemmas, discoveries, designs and desires. It emerges from our experiences with groups whose thoughtful feedback has helped us shape and hone the organization and presentation of the ideas found here.

Special thanks go to our talented technical team whose high standards, precision and diligence kept this project on course. Their special skills, reflected throughout this work, are much appreciated.

Katie O'Neill McCloskey, our language maven, sharpened our prose with her singular focus and knowledgeable copyedits.

Lynne Schueler, our compositor, set each page with skillful attention to detail.

Peggy Olcott, our slide designer, transferred her instructional design skills to add clarity to the presentation visuals.

June Lipton, our media master, orchestrated the various tasks necessary to upload and manage the web-based resources related to this book.

Michael Buckley illuminated the concepts and contents on the inside and the outside of this book with the gift of his visual intelligence. His spirit lives in these pages.

Contents

Contents *continued*

Contents *continued*

Celebrate success.   Learn from failure.   Acknowledge both.

About This Book

THIS book is based on the belief that groups that employ a repertoire of strategies and structures work more productively and time efficiently than any groups will without them. Strategies and protocols build capacity by providing guidelines and parameters that structure group interactions. They provide an organic base for behaviors that then become internally driven. That is, protocols become patterns, patterns become habits, and habits become norms.

This book is for group leaders and members of small groups that share leadership. Effective groups own their processes, actions and outcomes resulting in cooperation, coordination and shared understanding of procedures and protocols. Reliance on a single facilitator often inhibits group development. To spread skillfulness across the group and encourage more self-directed learning and monitoring behaviors by individual members, this book offers a rich palette of resources for teams. Shared tools and expectations help all group members increase their confidence; making facilitation a collective responsibility not a role.

Though meetings may be informal, they should never be casual. Thought, energy and intention must be put into design and preparation. The strategies in this book are easy to access, easy to follow and easy to apply by busy professionals.

What's Inside?

The **78** strategies offered here are organized into six functions to support purposeful process design: 1) activating, 2) assessing, goal setting and planning, 3) dialogue and discussion, 4) generating ideas, 5) summarizing and synthesizing, 6) text and information processing. These functions are arranged alphabetically and reflect the major activities that engage productive groups. Cohesive groups require tools to focus tasks and build relationships. Such processes encourage the interpersonal behaviors necessary for task success, such as listening for understanding, encouraging participation of all group members and balancing advocacy for one's own ideas with inquiry into the ideas of others.

While this book presents strategies within a specific function, a number of them can be applied to other functions. For example, many strategies for activating also serve to generate ideas and/or summarize. Although there is a section of strategies for generating ideas, many of the other strategies have a step that incorporates this function.

The strategies are formatted for ease of use. Each strategy page provides a variety of information for the group leader.

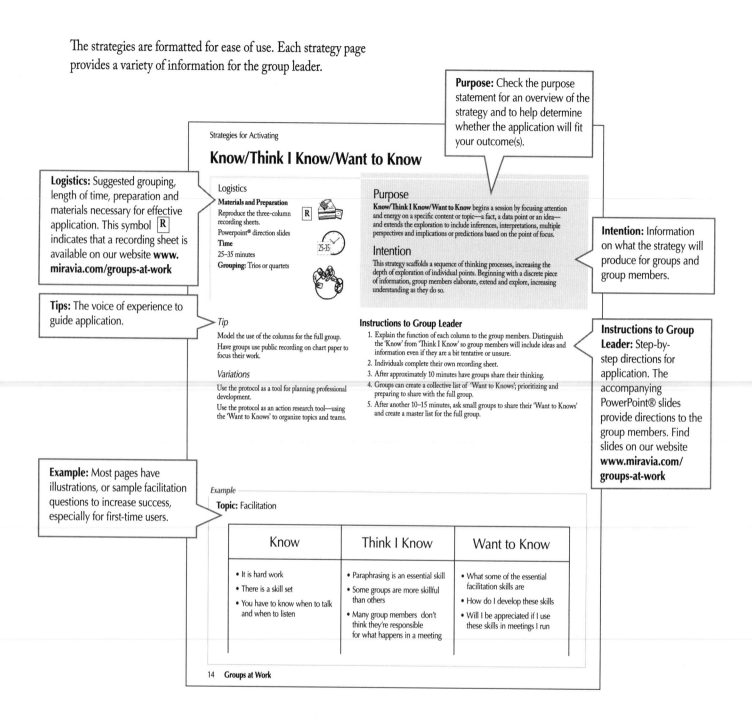

Purpose: Check the purpose statement for an overview of the strategy and to help determine whether the application will fit your outcome(s).

Logistics: Suggested grouping, length of time, preparation and materials necessary for effective application. This symbol [R] indicates that a recording sheet is available on our website **www.miravia.com/groups-at-work**

Tips: The voice of experience to guide application.

Intention: Information on what the strategy will produce for groups and group members.

Instructions to Group Leader: Step-by-step directions for application. The accompanying PowerPoint® slides provide directions to the group members. Find slides on our website **www.miravia.com/groups-at-work**

Example: Most pages have illustrations, or sample facilitation questions to increase success, especially for first-time users.

The strategy page shown includes:

Strategies for Activating

Know/Think I Know/Want to Know

Logistics

Materials and Preparation
Reproduce the three-column recording sheets.
Powerpoint® direction slides
Time
25–35 minutes
Grouping: Trios or quartets

Tip
Model the use of the columns for the full group.
Have groups use public recording on chart paper to focus their work.

Variations
Use the protocol as a tool for planning professional development.
Use the protocol as an action research tool—using the 'Want to Knows' to organize topics and teams.

Purpose
Know/Think I Know/Want to Know begins a session by focusing attention and energy on a specific content or topic—a fact, a data point or an idea—and extends the exploration to include inferences, interpretations, multiple perspectives and implications or predictions based on the point of focus.

Intention
This strategy scaffolds a sequence of thinking processes, increasing the depth of exploration of individual points. Beginning with a discrete piece of information, group members elaborate, extend and explore, increasing understanding as they do so.

Instructions to Group Leader
1. Explain the function of each column to the group members. Distinguish the 'Know' from 'Think I Know' so group members will include ideas and information even if they are a bit tentative or unsure.
2. Individuals complete their own recording sheet.
3. After approximately 10 minutes have groups share their thinking.
4. Groups can create a collective list of 'Want to Knows'; prioritizing and preparing to share with the full group.
5. After another 10–15 minutes, ask small groups to share their 'Want to Knows' and create a master list for the full group.

Example
Topic: Facilitation

Know	Think I Know	Want to Know
• It is hard work	• Paraphrasing is an essential skill	• What some of the essential facilitation skills are
• There is a skill set	• Some groups are more skillful than others	• How do I develop these skills
• You have to know when to talk and when to listen	• Many group members don't think they're responsible for what happens in a meeting	• Will I be appreciated if I use these skills in meetings I run

14   **Groups at Work**

Stacking Strategies and Agenda Design

Design matters. Productive sessions require thoughtful attention to matching process with purpose. To support process design, strategies can be "stacked" by function. For example, sequencing an activating strategy, a text processing strategy and a summarizing strategy provides an effective design for a 45–60 minute meeting. For extended timeframes, adding a dialogue or discussion strategy furthers the group's work. Selecting and sequencing strategies from the six functions named above creates effective and purposeful process designs. These strategy stacks save design time and produce productive, satisfying, high engagement sessions. See Table 1: Sample Strategy Stacks.

45-60 Minute Session	Topic: Collaboration
Activating: Help Wanted Ads	Help Wanted Ads for a skilled group member
Text and Information Processing: Say Something	Research synthesis or appropriate article
Summarizing and Synthesizing: Key Words	Individuals select and share key words from the session's reading and dialogue.

60-90 Minute Session	Topic: Improving Student Writing
Activating: Create a Recipe	Create a recipe for a productive writing lesson.
Dialogue and Discussion: Card Stack and Shuffle	Stems: Skillful student writers… Effective writing teachers…
Assessing, Planning and Goal Setting: Fishbone/Cause Effect Diagrams	Create diagrams analyzing factors that influence skillful student writing.
Summarizing and Synthesizing: Most Important Point	Individuals select a most important point

2-3 Hour Session	Topic: Formative Assessment
Activating: Reflect, Regroup, Return	Participants respond to and reflect on prompts about current assessment practices.
Text and Information Processing: Three A's Plus One	Participants read an article or sample chapter from a text. To save time this might be assigned prior to the session.
Generating Ideas: Color Question Brainstorming	Participants generate ideas and insights into improved assessment practices.
Summarizing and Synthesizing: Generate, Sort and Synthesize	Group members generate, sort and synthesize key ideas from the session.

Table 1: Sample Strategy Stacks

Designers consider the following questions when constructing a process agenda:

- How much time is available to achieve key outcomes?
- What ways does this group need to operate with this information/topic at this time?
- What cognitive processes or interactive patterns will be most productive?

Select from the strategies in this book to create a process design that answers these questions for your groups and group work.

Tips for Facilitators

This book provides a variety of strategies and protocols to support effective group work. These strategies fit within the larger field of orchestrating productive work sessions. Group members want to know two things: "Will this session be relevant to me?" and "Will my time be well spent?" Skilled facilitators signal their respect for these questions by being prepared, starting on time and outlining the purpose and design of the session. Their verbal and non-verbal actions communicate to group members that they are in good hands.

Facilitating group work is a complex yet learnable skill-set, requiring clarity of purpose, a repertoire of strategies, a verbal and nonverbal toolkit and the ability to read and adjust to the needs of the group. The tips below offer some facilitation fundamentals.

Introducing the Session

The opening sets the tone for the session. For both small and large groups, the first few minutes require intentional design and delivery. The ways in which a facilitator frames the purpose, task and process establishes receptivity and readiness for the work ahead.

Effective facilitators name the context within which the meeting occurs, along with the ways in which the process and products of that session mesh with each other and the wider frame. The time line, purpose, logistics and expectations are then clearly and explicitly stated.

Introducing a Strategy

Capturing the group members' attention and promoting their willingness to follow directions is a fundamental facilitation task. The basic pattern for accomplishing this task is to offer the *what, why* and *how* of structures, strategies and protocols. The "what" names the structure, strategy or protocol with which the group is about to engage. The "why" reveals the benefits of engaging as individuals and as a group. These might include efficient task completion, balanced participation, improved work products and opportunities to learn from and about each other. The "how" is the directions outlining steps for the procedures and processes.

Effective directions include modeling, specific examples and, in the case of complex or multi-step processes, visual support. Checking for understanding before proceeding will ensure that all group members are involved and will promote responsibility for accurately implementing the protocol. Each strategy in this book has related PowerPoint® slide(s) to support giving directions.

As a session progresses, facilitators create a pathway for group learning and group success by offering connections between strategies to create cohesive sessions. They do so by revisiting what has occurred (backtracking) and describing what is to come (foreshadowing) for both topics and processes. Group members' confidence increases when they have an orientation to the bigger picture and can track incremental accomplishments and project future experiences.

Fitting the Strategy to the Group

Strategies are most effective when structured intentionally to meet a specific group's needs, skill level and purposes. Thoughtfully structured strategies maximize the efficient use of time and increase the quality of both interactions and results. Novice groups require formal structures to scaffold success. More expert groups know how and when to structure a strategy to match the emotional and cognitive demands of their work.

Effective design includes three structuring variables: group size and composition, length of time and degree of structure. Designers use these elements to customize strategies to fit the specific requirements of the task, the group and the available timeframe.

TASK GROUP SIZE AND COMPOSITION. Using pairs, trios and quartets increases active participation and creates a climate for safe interaction. It is more efficient and manageable to subdivide large groups into smaller working units. The strategy descriptions that follow suggest an optimal group size. These small groups can be pre-assigned or randomly selected. (See Strategies for Forming Groups, page 91.)

In some cases, such as small grade-level teams or ad hoc committees, the trio or quartet is the group. In these circumstances, intentional design still matters and strategies should be modified accordingly.

Mixing members by same or different role, level of knowledge and degree of experience enriches the interaction and widens perspective related to tasks and topics. For example, groups can be organized as trios with each teacher from a different grade level or department, or by creating task groups whose experiences range from beginning teachers to seasoned veterans. When appropriate, task groups can combine to extend the conversation.

LENGTH OF TIME FOR A GROUP TO STAY TOGETHER. Small groups are effective for text-based tasks, idea generation and data exploration. By varying the length of time that groups work together and regrouping periodically, session participants develop deeper working relationships and greater knowledge of one another. Switching task group members also provides a period of purposeful movement for energy and brief social interaction. One pattern for intact groups is to establish base groups that meet regularly and employ informal grouping for designated tasks.

DEGREE OF STRUCTURE. Structuring choices involve materials, space, time, interaction patterns, and roles. Structure increases productivity and engagement. Some fundamental structures include recording publicly on chart paper so that all can see ideas and information, creating individual writing time and space before a conversation starts, providing individual recording sheets, using a round-robin-pattern for sharing ideas, using a public timer to guide processes and assigning roles, such as that of a reporter, a recorder, and a materials manager. Higher performing groups are not harmed by structure, and groups and group members that need structure will be greatly aided by it. (See Interaction Structures, page 89).

Without thoughtful choices to create the conditions for success, the strategies in this book become interesting activities and not purposeful processes.

In the Interest of Time

Time is our scarcest resource. Most groups have more task than time. Increasing time efficiency is a critical outcome for groups and group leaders. The strategies offered here can be modified to maximize meeting productivity. Several mini-management moves accomplish this purpose.

WORK OUTSIDE THE SESSION. Engaging with topics and tasks can begin before the meeting or work session and extend between sessions. For example, group members can read and annotate text, collect observations and examples of student work, complete stems related to the content, respond to a survey or set of questions, or record ideas on a structured worksheet. Using email, wikis, blogs and other technologies supports these activities. Having something in the hand, rather than just in the head, focuses the group and jumpstarts the session. Adaptations for using this time saver are described in many of the strategies that follow.

READY RESOURCES AND MATERIALS. Easy access to the tools necessary for group work saves time and energy and maintains attention and momentum. Preparing a central materials station or table tubs filled with highlight pens, index cards, sticky notes, felt markers, etc. are simple ways to achieve these outcomes. Other time savers include: arranging furniture for high engagement, posting chart paper prior to the meeting to create work stations and testing the technology when appropriate.

ASSIGN ROLES. Many strategies described in this book indicate the need for various roles. Groups expend time socially negotiating role selection, such as recorder or reporter. Group leaders save time by pre-determining or assigning these roles 'on the spot'.

DIVIDE THE TASK. Everyone doesn't have to do everything at the same time or together. Both tasks and strategies have natural sub-divisions. For example, small groups within the whole can explore different data sets, create scales and rubrics for different criteria, or read different and related pieces of text and then share their conclusions, work products or syntheses. Many of the strategies in this book can also be segmented. For example, each task group can be assigned different letters or sections of the alphabet when completing an alphabetical listing (see A-Z Listing, page 2).

Learning by Doing

We don't learn from experience, we learn by reflecting on our experiences. Learning groups and learning leaders preserve time and energy for reflecting on their processes and products and develop specific designs for this purpose.

Systematic experimentation with strategies and design elements in low-risk situations offers a trial run and the opportunity to refine facilitative practices. Tracking strategies and the results of their application supports adaptations based on observation, feedback and reflection. To serve this purpose you will find recording sheet masters on our website www.miravia.com/groups-at-work.

For leaders, stretching against comfort and style preferences provides opportunities to learn while meeting the needs of a broader spectrum of group members. For example, choosing strategies that may not be personally appealing often serves the learning needs of those with different preferences. Choose strategies from this book that will stretch your repertoire.

Groups also learn by applying similar processes for producing growth. Learning groups extend and refine their repertoire, stretch out of their comfort zones and modify behaviors by explicitly assessing successes and challenges. These groups expand their capacity to do more complex and challenging tasks, more collaboratively, more of the time.

Groups at Work

This book is a practical guide to structuring productive groups, providing strategies for conducting time-efficient, task-focused meetings. Thoughtful application of this toolkit will change the dynamic of your meetings resulting in greater satisfaction, stronger relationships and higher quality collaborative work.

We invite you to use this book as a resource for your own professional learning and as a guide to continual growth for your groups.

Laura Lipton   *Bruce Wellman*

Strategies for Activating

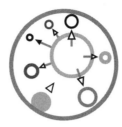

Getting individuals into the room physically, emotionally and cognitively prepared to work together—that is, to be a productive group—is a continual challenge. Well-chosen activators produce this readiness so that sessions begin on time, on task and on topic.

The activating strategies that follow engage prior knowledge, expand the individual and mutual knowledge base, and bring multiple perspectives to the surface. These tools are not warm-ups or icebreakers. Those insubstantial activities are intended to produce an affective outcome, which can be effectively achieved with strategies that also engage topic and task attention.

Activating strategies are often omitted for several reasons. One concern is time: the time required for designing productive interactions and the time consumed by adding processes to a tightly packed task agenda. Another concern is the perception that processes are pointless, waste energy and are inessential to the group's work. However, when activating processes are clearly and explicitly connected to purpose, these initial interactions become valued session elements.

For group leaders, the opening minutes of a meeting or work session are critical for establishing credibility and earning psychological permission to lead that event. By focusing attention and energy and establishing norms of participation, group leaders communicate respect for people's time and the contributions they will make to the group's work. Without effective activation, group members are often distracted by "life outside the room" and are not mentally or emotionally present, even if they are sitting at the table. Immediately applying structures that invite and balance participation sets the tone for shared engagement, and the likelihood that all members will contribute to the work-in-progress.

From a practical perspective, activating strategies provide a timely start, even if all members are not yet physically in place. Late arrivals are efficiently assimilated into the task, with minimal distraction. In addition, many of these strategies require group members to have pen, paper and other resources in hand, ready to work.

The strategies in this section offer a repertoire of effective options for starting the conversation.

NOTE: Many of the activating strategies described in this section can also be applied to summarize and synthesize.

A-Z Listing

Logistics

Materials and Preparation

Recording sheets with the alphabet written vertically down the left hand side or blank paper for participants to create their own form

One recording sheet or note paper per task group

PowerPoint® direction slides

Time: 15–20 minutes

Grouping: 2–6

Purpose

A-Z Listing uses the convention of the alphabet to focus the conversation and organize important ideas or key concepts. It is a time-efficient way to stimulate idea generation and encourage participation by all group members.

Intention

This interactive strategy is a quick idea generator to jumpstart thinking and idea development. It can also be used to activate or to review and reinforce previously explored information.

Tips

Model with one or two examples of appropriate completions, clearly indicating the expectation of full thoughts for each letter.

To save time, segment the alphabet and assign different sections to each task group, or ask groups to fill in at least 8–10 blanks, but not necessarily the entire alphabet.

Variations

Use A-Z Listing to process a piece of text.

Ask individual group members to do their A-Z Listing outside of a work session and bring it to the meeting to share and compare with others.

Use a chart paper and public recording to focus small group work.

Instructions to Group Leader

1. Create work groups (pairs or larger) and provide each group with a recording sheet.
2. Provide a topic and direct group members to fill in ideas or concepts related to that topic, with each idea beginning with a letter in the alphabet.
   Note: To save time, assign different sections of the alphabet to each group.
3. Be sure to reinforce that the information should be complete thoughts – not just words, as in an acrostic.
4. After a designated amount of time, ask each group to choose one idea to share.

Example

Topic: Effective Instruction

A _____

B _____

Create real life problems to solve

D _____

E _____

F _____

Give students partners to work with

H _____

I _____

J _____

K _____

L _____

M _____

N _____

Open-ended questions are most effective

Paraphrase students' contributions

Q _____

Reinforce previous learning

Set achievable, yet challenging goals for learners

Take time to pause and listen

Understanding should be assessed

V _____

W _____

X _____

Y _____

Z _____

Banned Words

Purpose

Banned Words is an activating strategy for starting a session and creating a sense of inclusion within the group. Banned words are those that are overused or have become meaningless. By naming "banned words" group members identify the buzz words in their work culture.

Intention

This strategy uses humor to focus and energize a group as a way to acknowledge potential resistance to any topics before the group. The pressure to avoid the banned words keeps group leaders alert and adds an element of playfulness to a session.

Instructions to Group Leader

1. Direct table groups to brainstorm a list of 8–10 terms that they would like banned from the session.
2. Groups then nominate selected items for recording on a master list to be posted visibly.
3. Ask the group to collectively groan whenever one of the banned words is used during the session.
4. Use one of the banned words in a sentence to have the group practice the groan.

Logistics

Materials and Preparation
Chart paper for master list
PowerPoint® direction slides
Time
10–15 minutes
Grouping: 4–6

Tips

Keep the brainstorming time tight to limit the possibility of storytelling and elaboration at the table groups.

To keep the group alert, periodically slip one of the banned words into a contextually appropriate sentence.

Variations

Have pairs do a rapid brainstorming of banned words before sharing them with their table groups.

Keep a running list of banned words and add to the list in subsequent sessions.

Bumper Stickers

Logistics

Materials and Preparation

Blank chart paper cut into strips

Several examples of traditional bumper stickers for demonstration

PowerPoint® direction slides

Time

10–12 minutes

Grouping: 3–6

Tips

It is useful to have several examples of traditional bumper stickers to get the group started.

Keep timeframes tight and use a public timer to keep groups focused on task completion.

Variations

Have groups create a slogan or logo for a T-shirt or a vanity license plate.

Purpose

Bumper Stickers is a high-energy strategy that uses symbolic thinking to focus the group's energy on the topic at hand. The creative aspect often adds humor and allows for high inclusion and acceptance of off-beat or novel ideas. Bumper Stickers is an effective choice to start or end a meeting or work session.

Intention

This strategy sparks conversation about a topic and establishes readiness for further exploration. It creates a vehicle for engaging more visually and artistically oriented group members.

Instructions to Group Leader

1. Explain that each table group will create a bumper sticker based on the topic being explored; creating a product that reflects some key aspect or big idea.

2. Let group members know that the time frame is intentionally brief (8–10 minutes) and that they may need to be ready with a draft, not a final product.

3. After the designated time, ask each group to choose a speaker to share its bumper sticker.

Example

Topic: Data Teams

Create a Recipe

Purpose

Create a Recipe is an engaging way to activate prior knowledge at the start of session or to summarize and synthesize ideas at the end of a session or session segment. In this strategy, table groups create recipes for such things as productive groups, successful lessons or skillful facilitation.

Intention

This strategy taps group members' personal and cultural knowledge of cooking and food preparation. This familiar schema provides a structure for efficiently generating criteria or qualities that would produce desired outcomes related to that group's topics and processes.

Instructions to Group Leader

1. Display a slide or chart with a word bank of terms related to food preparation and presentation.
2. Ask table groups to utilize the word banks to develop a recipe for the assigned topic.
3. Give a time for task completion, approximately 15 minutes.
4. At the end of the allotted time, invite table groups to select a spokesperson to share their draft recipe.

Logistics

Materials and Preparation

Slide or chart with word banks of recipe terms related to preparation, ingredients, measurement and presentation

Public Timer

PowerPoint® direction slides

Time

15–20 minutes depending on group size

Grouping: 2–6

Tips

Use a public timer to help keep groups on task.

Variations

Have table groups use a two-step process by first generating their own word banks and then drafting the recipe.

Example

Topic: Effective Groups

    Sample Word Bank:

      cup, pint, teaspoon, pinch, chop, mince, blend, fold, stir, bake, sauté, chill, grill, broil, serve on, spoon in, garnish with

EFFECTIVE GROUPS

4 C dialogue
3 C process strategies
1 C clear purpose
1 C open-ended questions
1 C paraphrase
½ C wait time
3 TBS humor

Gently stir first 3 ingredients. Fold in questions, paraphrase and wait time. Sprinkle with humor. Bake slowly for a year, checking frequently for group development.

Finding Common Ground

Logistics

Materials and Preparation

Public Timer

PowerPoint® direction slides

Time

5 minutes

Grouping: 4–6

Purpose

Finding Common Ground is an effective strategy for engaging a group, either at the start of a session or after regrouping.

Intention

This strategy sparks conversation and prepares a newly formed group for more complex and potentially more challenging work.

Tips

Even for group members that have known one another for some time, this strategy is an effective method for focusing social energy after a holiday break or between meetings.

Keep timeframes tight and use a public timer to keep groups focused on task completion.

Variations

Ask table groups to generate things they have in common related to the topic or their teaching practice (e.g., applications, concerns, questions, etc.).

Have groups generate commonalities for a particular period of time (e.g., during spring break, as a child, in undergraduate school).

Instructions to Group Leader

1. Explain that the table group task is to produce as many non-obvious things that the group members have in common as possible in a very tight time frame (3–5 minutes). Suggest to groups that they aim for a minimum of 3 items.

2. When time is called, each group chooses one commonality to share (e.g., we've all traveled somewhere in Asia). If others in the room share that attribute, they raise their hand, indicating affiliation with the group members who share the item.

First Word/Last Word

Purpose
First Word/Last Word is an adaptation of a traditional acrostic. Task groups generate full thoughts (phrases or sentences) that begin with each letter in the designated word. The word focuses the exploration of the topic under consideration.

Intention
This strategy surfaces and/or organizes important concepts, principles and understandings about a topic area.

Instructions to Group Leader

1. Determine a recorder for each task group.
2. Have recorders create a recording sheet or use a prepared recording sheet for capturing ideas.
3. Task groups generate ideas using language that expresses full thoughts that begin with each letter in the designated word and elaborate on important dimensions of the topic or concept being explored.
4. After 8–12 minutes, refocus for full group sharing and ask each task group to select one or two ideas to report.

Logistics

Materials and Preparation
Recording sheet with target word written horizontally down the left hand margin or blank paper
PowerPoint® direction slides

Time
8–12 minutes

Grouping: 4–6

Tips

To save time, assign different letters within the designated word(s) to different task groups. Suggest that they continue on with additional letters if time allows.

Rather than using a recording sheet, have groups do public charting, and post the charts for the view of other task groups.

Variations

Use this strategy to synthesize a piece of text.

Use the alphabet to prompt idea generations, rather than a specific word and follow directions above. (See A-Z Listing, page 2)

Example

Topic: Data Teams

D etermines direction for future planning

A ction research provides data that informs instruction

T akes a group to fully mine, analyze and interpret results

A ssessments should be both formative and summative

Give One to Get One

Logistics

Materials and Preparation

Index or blank note cards

Topics, sentence stems or questions

PowerPoint® direction slides

Time

15 minutes

Grouping: 4–6

Purpose

Give One to Get One sets up an exchange of information in preparation for further exploration. It can be applied to a wide range of topics, including information about group members' interests and experiences.

Intention

This interactive strategy provides physical energy and surfaces individual perspectives, knowledge and experience. It creates a shared base of information for further processing by the group members.

Tips

Add an explicit direction to paraphrase the information being exchanged for application of this important skill.

To save meeting time, group members can bring their completed Give One cards to the meeting.

Variations

When a group is meeting for the first time, add identity information to the card (e.g., name, role, work site).

Use this protocol for participants to reflect on their growth as a group. For example, "One way the group added to my learning…"; or "What is one contribution you made to the group's productivity during this session?"

Instructions to Group Leader

1. Direct individuals to fill in a card with an answer to a question, a completion to a sentence stem or an association with a topic.

2. Once the cards are complete, direct group members to circulate around the room, sharing the information on their card and then *exchanging* cards with their colleague. NOTE: Individuals leave with the colleague's card.

3. After two or three exchanges, direct group members to return to their table and share the information on the card they have in hand.

4. Table groups identify themes and patterns to share with the full group.

Example

Sample Prompts:

One success I've experienced with our new math curriculum …

One assumption for me in working with data …

What is the most important skill for an effective reader?

Go to Your Corners

Purpose

Go to Your Corners is a strategy used for group members to assess their interest in major themes, outcomes or key issues in a meeting or work session. Go to Your Corners can also be used to review and/or summarize key ideas at the close of a session.

Intention

This strategy connects group members with content, concepts and issues by providing them with a sense of the relative interests and concerns of their colleagues. Purposeful physical movement also provides energy and focus.

Instructions to Group Leader

1. Describe the purpose of this strategy and the content or issue in each corner.
2. Structure a period of quiet reflection. Then ask participants to move to the corner of greatest interest to them.
3. Have each corner group subdivide into clusters of 2–3 to share and explore their reasons for choosing that theme or issue.
4. After a designated amount of time, invite group members to share some of their thinking about the reasons for their choice of corner with the full group.
5. Have group members move to their second choice corner and repeat the clustering, exploring and sharing processes.

Logistics

Materials and Preparation

Charts labeled and posted in corners of the room listing essential concepts or categories related to the meeting or session content or outcomes

PowerPoint® direction slides

Time

15–20 minutes

Grouping: Full group

Tips

Create a handout with brief descriptions of the essential content or factors related to each corner theme. Have participants read and clarify their understanding of these ideas before moving to their corners of interest.

At selected points in a session or in subsequent sessions have participants revisit their corners of choice to review and clarify their understandings.

Variations

Combine with Spend-a-Buck (see page 33) to help individuals activate their thinking in preparation for selecting corners.

Example

Topic: Leading Groups

Project Planning

Group Development

Facilitation Skills

Presentation Skills

Grounding

Logistics

Materials and Preparation

Slide or chart with grounding prompts to display

Chairs arranged in a circle or people seated around a table or tables

PowerPoint® direction slides

Time

15–20 minutes depending on group size

Grouping: 8–15

Tip

Grounding is a valuable beginning activity for a newly formed task group, especially when it is a mixed group that does not work together regularly.

Variation

If the group contains more than 16 people, create two smaller groups. Have the person who goes first in each circle offer a summary to the larger group of the key points that emerged in his or her respective grounding circle upon return to the larger group.

Purpose

Grounding uses a round-robin pattern (see page 89) for starting a meeting or work session. Given several prompts, each participant verbally responds while all other participants listen without interruption or comment. Grounding provides a safe way for participants to share their thoughts and feelings about a topic, session or the group itself. It provides information to the group leader about the emotional and cognitive climate of the group.

Intention

This strategy sets a tone of respect, balanced participation and focused listening. It honors individual perspectives by establishing a place at the table for each participant in the session.

Instructions to Group Leader

1. Seat the group in a circle so that all participants have a full view of one another.
2. Display a chart or slide with the grounding prompts and request a period of silence for group members to form their responses.
3. Describe the round-robin pattern that the group will follow:
   - Participants talk in turn.
   - All others remain silent and give full attention to each speaker.
4. Designate the starting speaker.
5. After everyone has spoken, offer a summary of key points, any themes that emerged, and any critical differences in expectations.

Example

> Name …
>
> Relation to this topic …
> Expectations for this work …
> How I feel about being here today …

> Name …
>
> Payoffs for task success …
> Hopes for what might be accomplished today …
> Concerns about what might happen here today …

Group Résumé

Purpose

Group Résumé is an effective strategy for beginning table group engagement, either at the start of a session or after regrouping. The short time frame and need for collaboration create high engagement and focused social energy.

Intention

This strategy sparks conversation and prepares a newly formed group for more complex and potentially more challenging work. Team reports give the whole group an idea of who is in the room.

Logistics

Materials and Preparation

Chart paper and felt-tip markers

PowerPoint® direction slides

Time

Approximately 15 minutes

Grouping: 4–6

Instructions to Group Leader

1. Explain that the table group task is to create a résumé for the group, including various categories of information, as follows:

   GROUP NAME OR TITLE

   Background

   Interests/Hobbies

   Some things you might guess about us

   Some things that might surprise you

   Signatures

2. After a designated amount of time, have each group share highlights from their résumé.

Tips

Give teams a time cue before they organize their report and have them identify a reporter or mode of reporting.

Keep timeframes tight and use a public timer to keep groups focused on task completion.

Variation

Ask table groups to generate information related to the topic (e.g., things we agree with, disagree with, have applied).

Example

> **Group Résumé**
>
> Experienced K-12, with an emphasis in Spec Ed, L.A. & Science Ed
>
> Music, birdwatching, photography, hiking
>
> Travel widely, avid readers
>
> Have had physical contact with 3 species of marine mammals
>
> *Laura*, **Bruce**, Tanesha, *Raul*, *Maria*

Help Wanted Ads

Logistics

Materials and Preparation

Note and/or chart paper

PowerPoint® direction slides

Time

Approximately 15 minutes

Grouping: 3–6

Purpose

Help Wanted Ads is an engaging strategy for starting a meeting or work session that uses a well-known template to focus the group's energy on the topic. The creative aspect promotes high inclusion and encourages both clever and amusing characteristics. Help Wanted Ads is also an effective choice to end a meeting or work session.

Intention

This strategy sparks conversation about a topic and establishes readiness for further exploration. It creates a vehicle for recalling important information at the start of a session or summarizing key ideas at the end of a session.

Tips

It is useful to first have group members generate a word and phrase bank of typical help wanted ad vocabulary.

Keep timeframes tight and use a public timer to keep groups focused on task completion.

Variations

If the larger group will be working with the selected topic over time, have table groups create a chart and post their help wanted ad on the wall.

Instructions to Group Leader

1. Explain that each table group will create a help wanted ad based on the topic being explored, creating a product that reflects some key aspect or big idea.

2. Let group members know that the time frame is intentionally brief (8–10 minutes) and that they may need to be ready with a draft, not a final product.

3. After the designated time, ask each group to choose a speaker to share its help wanted ad.

Example

Topic: Skillful Group Member

Wanted-Skillful Group Member

Must have disposition and skills for collaboration including: deep listening abilities, paraphrasing skills, willingness to suspend judgment and a spirit of inquiry. Sense of humor is highly valued. Send résumé and video of yourself participating in a meeting to www.joingroup.org

Just Like Me!

Purpose

Just Like Me! provides energy and information about the group by asking group members to stand and identify themselves saying "just like me," if a particular criteria or experience that is named is true for them.

Intention

This strategy works to create greater group cohesion as members discover common experiences and characteristics. It also provides key information to the group leader regarding roles, interests and experience for later reference and planning.

Logistics

Materials and Preparation

A list of statements appropriate for your group/ location

PowerPoint® direction slides

Time

Approximately 15 minutes

Grouping: Full group

Instructions to Group Leader

1. Explain to group members that you are going to name an experience, interest or characteristic, and if it is true for them, they stand and say "just like me" and look around the room to see who else in the group has that same thing in common with them.

2. Call out several statements, pausing between items to allow group members to scan for who is standing. Items that include preferences, recent experiences, role-related information, and professional or personal qualities make effective choices.

Tip

Be sure to share the "what, why, how" of this strategy, as it is a stretch for some group members.

Variations

Have group members generate the Just Like Me! statements for each other.

Use Just Like Me! to check for content understandings. For example, "I can give you one example of a routine that works for primary students," or "I know an effective strategy for literacy development." Then randomly select some participants to share their response.

Example

Professional:

I've taught in the same district for my whole career.

I've been in education for more than 10 years/less than 3 years.

I am a mentor of first-year teachers.

I have a love/hate relationship with data.

Personal:

I love chocolate.

I am an only child/or the oldest of my siblings.

My favorite activities involve things at home.

I am a pet owner.

I have added someone new to my family in the last year.

Know/Think I Know/Want to Know

Logistics

Materials and Preparation

Reproduce the three-column recording sheets.

PowerPoint® direction slides

Time

25–35 minutes

25-35

Grouping: Trios or quartets

Tips

Model the use of the columns for the full group.

Have groups use public recording on chart paper to focus their work.

Variations

Use the protocol as a tool for planning professional development.

Use the protocol as an action research tool—using the "Want to Knows" to organize topics and teams.

Purpose

Know/Think I Know/Want to Know begins a session by focusing attention and energy on a specific content or topic—a fact, a data point or an idea—and extends the exploration to include inferences, interpretations, multiple perspectives and implications or predictions based on the point of focus.

Intention

This strategy scaffolds a sequence of thinking processes, increasing the depth of exploration of individual points. Beginning with a discrete piece of information, group members elaborate, extend and explore, increasing understanding as they do so.

Instructions to Group Leader

1. Explain the function of each column to the group members. Distinguish the "Know" from "Think I Know" so group members will include ideas and information even if they are a bit tentative or unsure.

2. Individuals complete their own recording sheet.

3. After approximately 10 minutes have groups share their thinking.

4. Groups can create a collective list of "Want to Knows"; prioritizing and preparing to share with the full group.

5. After another 10–15 minutes, ask small groups to share their "Want to Knows" and create a master list for the full group.

Example

Topic: Facilitation

Know	Think I Know	Want to Know
• It is hard work • There is a skill set • You have to know when to talk and when to listen	• Paraphrasing is an essential skill • Some groups are more skillful than others • Many group members don't think they're responsible for what happens in a meeting	• What some of the essential facilitation skills are • How I develop these skills • Whether I'll be appreciated if I use these skills in meetings I run

Looking Back/Looking Ahead

Purpose

Looking Back/Looking Ahead provides an effective way to expand group members' time horizons and increase receptivity to a new initiative. By recalling a time period in the past and projecting toward a specific time in the future, group members gain perspective and insight into both the positive and negative influences of change.

Intention

This strategy creates readiness for exploring a change initiative by widening perspectives for individuals and the group. It is a psychologically safe yet provocative conversation starter that honors individual viewpoints, while promoting group focus and energy.

Logistics

Materials and Preparation

Recording sheets with three columns or blank note paper
PowerPoint® direction slides

Time

15–20 minutes

Grouping: 4–6

Instructions to Group Leader

1. Ask each participant, working individually, to complete each column in the recording sheet: things that have changed since they were 12 years old (technologically, sociologically and in schools); things that have stayed the same; and things that they imagine will be common 12 years in the future.
   Note: 12 years is used because it is the approximate length of time children stay within most school systems.

2. Once individuals have completed their recording sheets, structure table group discussion. Offer question prompts, such as:

   What strikes you as you share and compare?

   What are some patterns you are noticing?

   What are some implications for your/our work?

Tip

Group members can complete their Looking Back/ Looking Ahead recording sheet on their own and bring it to the session.

Variations

Instead of a period of time, change the columns to reflect group members roles. For example, "What has changed since you first became a teacher?" "What has stayed the same?" "What do you imagine will be common twelve years from now for the teachers who are new to the profession?"

Instead of recording sheets, ask group members to find something in their pocket (or purse) that would not have been there 12 years ago to launch a similar discussion.

Example

Topic: Technology in the Classroom

Things that have changed since you were 12 years old:	Things that have stayed the same since you were 12 years old:	Things that will be common 12 years from now:
Technological Sociological Schools	Technological Sociological Schools	Technological Sociological Schools
Computers Cell phones Internet access Web Resources Digital Whiteboards Email Videoconferencing Social networking Cyberbullying Facebook Friends Text Messaging Data access	Photocopiers that break Projected images for kids to read and take notes Teacher directed use of technology Need to connect with friends Better technology use outside of school than inside Budget constraints	Total wireless access everywhere Universal tablet devices Student centered learning with technology – anytime anyplace Global collaboration – students without borders Artificial intelligence driven personal learning platforms that adapt to the learner

Strategies for Activating

Paired Verbal Fluency

Logistics

Materials and Preparation
PowerPoint® direction slides

Time
5 minutes

Grouping: Pairs

Purpose

Paired Verbal Fluency structures a quick verbal exchange about a topic prior to, or after exploring it. It is an effective method for activating readiness and confidence before exploring data or text-based information. This strategy can also be used to summarize and synthesize at the end of a session.

Intention

This strategy provides a low-risk structure for surfacing information. The need to construct language quickly and to listen to another's ideas stimulates and challenges thinking and helps surface knowledge about the topic at hand.

Tips

Give a minute of think time after announcing the topic, so participants can be ready to share.

Let group members know that the time is very brief, intentionally, as the strategy is designed to prime the pump before deeper exploration of the topic.

Variation

Vary the time segments by lengthening the rounds (e.g., 90, 60, 45 seconds) or reversing the pattern.

Instructions to Group Leader

1. Ask partners to letter-off A and B to create pairs of one A and one B.
2. Assign a topic and explain that each partner will be speaking about that topic in turn, and without interruption.
3. Partners listen carefully to each other, and during their own turn cannot repeat anything that was previously said.
4. At the start signal, A begins. After the elapsed time, say "Switch" and B takes over. Partners alternate turns at your signal for three rounds, as follows:

   Round One: 60 seconds each

   Round Two: 45 seconds each

   Round Three: 30 seconds each

Reflect, Regroup, Return

Purpose

Reflect, Regroup, Return is a reflective and interactive process for starting a meeting or learning session. After responding in writing to several prompts, participants leave their home groups and form clusters of 3–4 to engage in dialogue about their ideas, and then return to their home group with themes and patterns from their interactions.

Intention

This strategy establishes norms of balanced participation and focused listening, providing a safe way for sharing thoughts and ideas related to selected topics and learning goals. The protocol widens perspectives and increases understanding of the others' viewpoints. It is an intellectually and emotionally engaging activity for thoughtful groups, especially if participants have had some experiences with the verbal and nonverbal patterns of purposeful dialogue.

Logistics

Materials and Preparation

Slide or chart displayed with reflection prompts

Recording sheets with chosen prompt questions

Public Timer

PowerPoint® direction slides

Time

30–40 minutes

Grouping: 4–6

Instructions to Group Leader

1. Distribute the recording sheets and or reveal the prompts on a chart or slide.
2. Set a time period for participants to record their responses. Name this period as a time for silence to protect the space for reflection.
3. Invite participants to move away from their table groups and form dialogue groups of 3–4 people. Emphasize that the outcome of this grouping is to understand the perspectives and thinking of others and not to agree or disagree with their ideas.
4. After the designated dialogue time, ask these small groups to summarize the themes and main ideas in their interactions.
5. Have participants return to their home groups and share the themes that emerged from their respective dialogue groups.
6. Invite table groups to share these themes with the larger group.

Tips

Use the directions slide or chart paper to reveal one prompt at a time, especially if the prompts build on one another and get increasingly personal.

Be sure to balance group size at each table.

Choose three or four prompts that will produce the richest engagement.

Adjust the number of prompts to your group's readiness and your time frame.

Example

Sample Prompts:

What are some of the commitments that brought you into this room?

What are some of the costs for your being here today?

How valuable do you think this work might be?

What are some of the crossroads you are facing (in your work or with this project)?

What are some of the things you are complaining about (in your work or related to this project)?

What are some of your contributions to the very things you are complaining about?

What might be some of the things that you or your (team/staff/group) know that nobody else knows about this work (or project)?

Sample prompts adapted from Block, 2008.

Since Last We Met

Logistics

Materials and Preparation

Public Timer

PowerPoint® direction slides

Time

10–15 minutes

Grouping: 4–6

Purpose

Since Last We Met engages and reconnects an ongoing group, especially when there has been a significant time gap since their previous session. Each table group member reflects on the prompt and in turn offers a response. Table groups then select one response to share with the larger group.

Intention

This strategy eases the transition back into the working group and supports group members in acknowledging the many demands that they all face in their personal and work lives. Responses are often humorous which adds to the focusing quality of the experience and strengthens relationships among group members.

Tips

Use a public timer to help keep groups on task.

Variations

Offer specific genres to deepen the analogies. For example,

"Since last we met, life has been like what movie or television genre?"

- action/adventure
- sports
- reality show
- game show
- horror
- science fiction
- romantic comedy
- family comedy

Make the prompt specific to that group's work or roles.

For example, "since last we met, my classroom has been like…"

or, "since last we met my school has been like…"

Instructions to Group Leader

1. Display a slide or chart with the prompt, "Since last we met, life has been like what book, movie or song title?"

2. Give table group members a moment to reflect and choose their response.

3. Have table groups use a round-robin pattern to share their responses with one another.

4. Table groups then select one response to share with the larger group.

Example

Since we last met, life has been like *Seinfeld* because weird personalities have dominated my days.

Since we last met, life has been like *The Grapes of Wrath* because I'm living in a dustbowl, struggling to survive.

Since we last met, life has been like "Yellow Submarine" because our PLC is really coming together.

Synectics

Purpose

Synectics engages and focuses the group's energy at the beginning of a session. The combination of brainstorming and metaphorical thinking allows for high inclusion and acceptance of offbeat or novel ideas. Synectics is also an effective choice to end a meeting or work session.

Intention

This strategy is a low-risk way to spark conversation about a topic and establish readiness for further exploration. It also provides a vehicle for all voices to be included.

Logistics

Materials and Preparation

One slide with one or more visual images or several cards with a variety of images to be distributed to each table

PowerPoint® direction slides

Time

Approximately 15 minutes

Grouping: 3–6

Instructions to Group Leader

1. Display a visual image on the screen, or supply picture cards on each table (these can be the same image, or different illustrations at each table).
2. Explain that the task is to complete the stem: "This topic is like this image because…" and generate and record as many comparisons between the image displayed and the topic presented as possible in the time allotted.
3. Be sure each group has a recorder, and establish a brainstorm protocol: multiple comparisons generated, all ideas accepted.
4. After three minutes of brainstorming, ask the group to pause. Foreshadow that each group will choose one comparison to share out loud, and offer one more minute for each group to make their choice.
5. Focus the group for sharing.

Tips

Reinforce that brainstorming is acceptance of all ideas and ask groups to self-monitor if they're getting bogged down with explanations.

Encourage task groups to make a back-up choice when getting ready for the full group share; especially when you are using one image for everyone.

Variations

In addition to making comparisons, groups can also generate contrasts: "This topic is NOT like this image because…"

Give groups a category or an individual item (without an illustration) for brainstorming comparisons. "This topic is like this item because…" or, "This topic is like something in this category because…"

Place an object or several objects on each table (or ask group members to find something in their pocket and invite them to make comparisons between a topic and the object(s)).

Example

Topic: Skilled Leadership

Skilled leadership is like  because …

it can be hit or miss

it takes a team

you can get increasingly skillful

you don't have to be perfect to have a good batting average

you do it in public

Think & Write/Pair & Share

Logistics

Materials and Preparation

Index cards or note paper

PowerPoint® direction slides

Time

8–10 minutes

Grouping: Pairs

Purpose

Think & Write/Pair & Share structures individual think time with a partnered exchange. It is extremely versatile and can be applied to a wide variety of topics in a wide variety of contexts. The paired exchange creates readiness for further exploration of a topic.

Intention

This strategy balances participation and provides a low-risk, time-efficient method for shared exploration. Individual preparation time increases the confidence of each partner and the quality of the exchange. The written notes increase focus and momentum when partners begin their conversations.

Tips

Provide an overview of the three steps so that participants know they will be sharing their response with at least one other person.

To preserve meeting time, ask participants to prepare and bring their notes with them.

Variations

Once partners have exchanged and explored their Think & Writes, form quartets (pairs squared), or larger groups for further discussion.

Instructions to Group Leader

1. Give group members a prompt, stem or question to think and write about.

2. After 2 minutes or so, form partners. These can be based on proximity, predetermined, or organized in the moment. (See Strategies for Forming Groups, page 91.)

3. Partners share their responses.

Example

Sample Prompts:

What is one thing you do to engage your staff during meetings?

What is one key element for a positive classroom environment?

What is one assumption you have about using formative assessments with students?

What kinds of thinking are embedded in math problem solving?

Strategies for Assessing, Goal Setting and Planning

"Ready, fire, aim" is the modus operandi of many groups. Both simple and more complex processes for determining present state and next steps—short and long term—are necessary to support group reflection and shared commitment to goals.

Groups that are too busy to reflect and plan are too busy to learn and improve. Structuring reflection—affective and cognitive, personal and collective—makes the difference between groups stuck in a rut and groups that grow. Templates for goal setting and tools for planning increase clarity of purpose, energy for taking on difficult tasks and confidence in these undertakings.

Success requires action that is cohesive and goal-focused. Agreed upon, understood and shared success criteria and clear standards for practice serve as points of reference for determining progress. Whether these criteria are generated by the group or externally imposed, effective strategies for applying them are critical. Explicit scaffolds for planning focus energy and minimize verbal excursions into irrelevant details.

Many groups confuse action with outcome. Doing something feels better than systematically researching an issue before determining goals. In addition, differing work style preferences can create impatience, conflict and tension about the best use of meeting time. Time and energy are diverted when group members differ in their value for reflection over quick decisions, or refining details versus exploring the bigger picture.

Monitoring the progress of group member capacities, as well as plans of action, matters. Strategies that produce clear goals and data-driven plans increase the internal and external accountability necessary for success.

The strategies in this book for assessing, goal setting and planning bring outcomes and explicit success criteria to the center of the conversation.

NOTE: In contrast with the other sections in this book, this section contains strategies with related but distinct purposes. Consider applying several strategies within this section in sequence for a planning or decision-making session.

Fishbone/Cause-Effect Diagrams

Logistics

Materials and Preparation

Chart paper and colored markers for each group

Sticky Notes

PowerPoint® direction slides

Time

30–40 minutes

Grouping: 4–6 or full group

Tips

Caution the group against the temptation to tell stories and share too many examples while they are brainstorming and organizing the diagrams.

Apply think-pair-share or round-robin patterns (see page 89) to balance participation and encourage full engagement by all group members.

You can use sticky notes at the brainstorming and categorizing stage to encourage idea production and flexibility in grouping related ideas.

Variation

Divide up the categories and have each small group do a first-draft brainstorming for their assigned area.

Purpose

Fishbone/Cause-Effect Diagrams visually represent the relationships between a particular effect and its potential causes. This tool is particularly useful when groups need to identify, analyze and isolate the underlying causes of a vexing problem or existing conditions in a group, organization or project. Kaoru Ishikawa, a pioneer of quality management processes in the Kawasaki shipyards, originally conceived the Fishbone or Cause-Effect Diagram as a problem-solving tool for developing understanding within project groups.

Intention

This graphic tool provides a focusing point for the conversation and organizes the thinking of group members. The physical production of the graphic organizer creates a high level of interaction and displays the dynamics of interrelated elements in a system. This tool increases the capacities of group members to view a problem through a system's lens. Most importantly, it focuses on causes—not symptoms.

Instructions to Group Leader

1. Identify a condition or problem for which the group will be generating possible causes. Note: The group may have previously identified the issue or topic.

2. Have group members brainstorm possible causes of the identified topic.

3. Group the causes into 4–6 major categories. Note: In some cases it is useful to provide the category labels first and then have group members generate ideas within the categories.

4. Construct the Fishbone Diagram or have each table group construct its own as follows:

   a. Place the problem statement in a box at the right side of the chart (the head of the fish). Draw a straight line, or spine, from the head to the tail.

   b. Draw one fishbone for each category angled away from the spine. Place a major causal category label in a box at the end of each fishbone.

   c. Fill in the specific causes related to each category along each fishbone. Note: It is possible for a specific cause to be placed in more than one category.

5. Review each of the elaborated causal categories. Circle the specific causes that are most likely the major contributors to the problem being considered.

6. Assign task groups to develop plans for addressing selected areas of concern. (See Outcome Mapping, page 29.)

Example

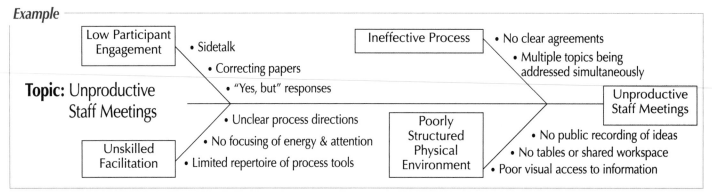

Force Field Analysis

Purpose

Force Field Analysis is a visual tool for analyzing the forces that drive and impede some change or process you wish to implement. This tool was developed by the social psychologist Kurt Lewin for analyzing the dynamics of systems to see what keeps conditions in place and what might need to change to alter those conditions. Use this tool to identify driving forces (pros) and restraining forces (cons) related to the issue at hand. Then consider what might need to happen to amplify the driving forces and mitigate the restraining forces.

Intention

This graphic tool provides a focusing point for the conversation and develops a system's view of problems and issues. This tool offers perspective for change processes, implementation issues and decision-making groups.

Instructions to Group Leader

1. Identify an implementation issue or goal the group would like to achieve. List this on the top of the chart paper.
2. Draw a line down the center of the paper and label the left hand column "Driving Forces" and the right hand column "Restraining Forces."
3. Brainstorm and record the driving forces in the left hand column.
4. Brainstorm and record the restraining forces in the right hand column.
5. Examine the lists and explore the validity of these forces, their significance, their relative strengths and weaknesses, and the potential for modifying any of these.
6. Assign a strength rating score to each item on each list (1 for low – 5 for high).
7. Tally the columns to assess the degree of balance in the opposing forces.
8. Select specific driving forces that might be amplified to increase their influence.
9. Select specific restraining forces that might be addressed to reduce their influence.
10. Assign working groups to address the selected forces.

Logistics

Materials and Preparation

Chart paper and colored markers for each group

PowerPoint® direction slides

Time

30–40 minutes

Grouping: 4–6 or full group

Tips

If the restraining forces are significantly greater than the driving forces, change may not be possible.

Apply think-pair-share or round-robin patterns to balance participation and encourage full engagement by all group members.

Variations

Separate working groups and assign one to brainstorming the driving forces and one to brainstorming the restraining forces.

Why did you make change? What's holding you back?

Example

Issue: Implementing a New Middle School Math Program

Driving Forces	Restraining Forces
Not enough students prepared for high school math courses	Lack of teacher dissatisfaction
Outdated Materials	Need for extensive teacher training
Need for technology integration	Expensive support materials
Low state assessment scores	Parents of high-performing students resisting program changes
Lack of student engagement	Lack of coaching capacity to support teachers during change process
Need for applied math/project-based materials	Need for sufficient technological infrastructure to support new program
Parent pressure	

Futures Wheel

Logistics

Materials and Preparation

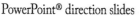

Chart paper/chart stands or wall stations or a futures wheel recording sheet for each participant or pair

PowerPoint® direction slides

45-60

Time

45–60 minutes

Grouping: 4–6

Tip

It is useful to model a wheel with a group that is using this protocol for the first time.

Variations

Instead of an event or issue, place a question in the center of the wheel.

Have pairs create their own wheel and then work with a larger group of six to eight to combine their thinking. You might organize job- or experience-alike pairs and then establish a more diverse working group.

Purpose

Futures Wheel is a graphic tool for forecasting ripple effects, both positive and negative, resulting from an event or initiative. The Futures Wheel is an effective launching point for study groups or task forces.

Intention

This strategy incorporates diverse, creative and inventive thinking. It honors individual viewpoints while widening perspectives for each and all group members. It also illustrates the notion that any event has both potentially positive and negative effects and helps to reduce impulsive jumps to short-term solutions.

Instructions to Group Leader

1. Write the name of the event, innovation or issue at the center of the wheel.

2. Work outward to the first layer of the circle, indicating that there are two negative effects and two positive effects in this layer. Explain that the negatives and positives should be as diverse as possible from one another.

3. Next, proceed to the second layer. Explain that each negative outcome and each positive outcome leads to its own negative and positive ripple effect.

4. Move outward to the third layer using the same process. Give participants an opportunity to examine and discuss the results at this point. Identify the most positive and most negative ripple effects that emerge at the third layer.

5. Depending on the topics, group members can now explore potential changes in policy, or brainstorm options for amplifying the positive effects and minimizing the negative effects.

Example

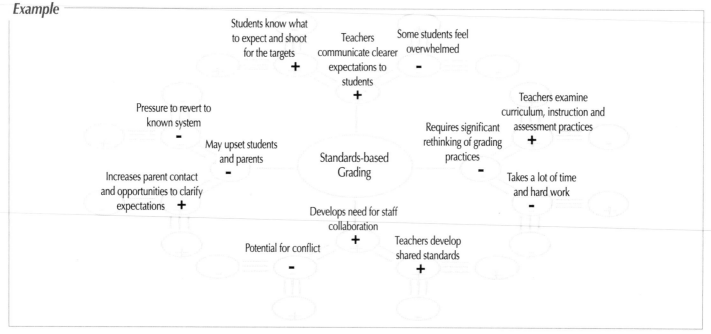

Got It! Need It!

Purpose

Got It! Need It! uses a two column structure for participant self-assessment, before or after a work or training session. Got It! Need It! can be used for conceptual understandings, information or skills related to a topic or school improvement initiative.

Intention

This reflective strategy is an efficient way to begin a plan of action, or a commitment to applying new practices. It provides individual think time, as well as a structure to focus sharing.

Logistics

Materials and Preparation

Recording sheet with two columns labeled "Got It!" and "Need It!" or blank note paper

PowerPoint® direction slides

Time

15–20 minutes

Grouping: 2–6

Instructions to Group Leader

1. Create work groups (pairs or larger), with a recording sheet for each group.
2. Ask group members to work individually first, completing their recording sheet determining ideas, skills or knowledge that they've "got" and those that they "need" to increase their confidence or effectiveness.
3. After a designated amount of time, structure interaction or full group exploration of the individual responses.

Tip

Group members can complete their Got It! Need It! recording sheet on their own and bring it to the session.

Variations

Use the Got It! Need It! format electronically and share online.

Use the completed Got It! Need It! recording sheets to focus one-to-one or small group planning conversations.

Example

Topic: Coaching Skills

Got it!	Need it!
Listen to understand	Paraphrase more
Physical alignment	Posture / gesture match
Fewer judgments	Ask more than tell

Here's What!/So What?/Now What?

Logistics

Materials and Preparation

Three-column recording sheets with "Here's What!" items identified

PowerPoint® direction slides

Time

20–30 minutes

20-30

Grouping: Trios or quartets

Tip

Use public recording on chart paper to focus group work.

Variations

Have each group work on a different set of "Here's What!" items.

Have one group create the "Here's What!" items for another group.

Use the protocol as a planning tool. Place an issue or concern in the "Here's What!" column; its implications in the "So What?" column; and potential actions in the "Now What?" column.

Purpose

Here's What!/So What?/Now What? is a versatile strategy that focuses attention and energy on a specific piece of information—a fact, a data point or an idea—and extends the exploration to include inferences, interpretations, multiple perspectives and implications or predictions based on the point of focus.

Intention

This strategy scaffolds a sequence of thinking processes, increasing the depth of exploration of individual points. Beginning with a discrete piece of information, group members elaborate, extend and explore, increasing understanding as they do so.

Instructions to Group Leader

1. Explain the function of each column to the group members. Items for the "Here's What!" column include specific facts, data points or discrete pieces of information generated by group members. In the "So What?" column are interpretations or inferences based on the first column. The "Now What?" column follows with implications, predictions or next steps.

2. Provide specific "Here's What!" items for the group, or ask group members to generate items related to the topic being explored or their observations of a data set.

3. Direct task groups (trios or quartets) to work across the column to complete the recording sheet.

4. After a designated amount of time, organize a full group discussion.

Example

Here's What!	So What?	Now What?
50% of Grade 8 students meet or exceed the standards for reading comprehension.	What we're doing is working for some but not all of our students.	We need to expand our repertoire of explicit instructional strategies in grades 6-8 for teaching important comprehension skills.

If... Then...

Purpose

If... Then... is a time-efficient method for envisioning the application of a new idea or practice. It provides an opportunity for each group member to weigh the information from a session and distill aspects that would make a positive difference in their own work.

Intention

This strategy gives individual group members a chance to consider the impact of new ideas or applications on their own practice and offers a concise way to encourage a commitment to growth. It provides choice in determining short-term goals and the opportunity to contextualize the concepts explored in a learning session.

Instructions to Group Leader

1. Distribute recording sheets or cards and ask individuals to complete the stems: If I remember to... Then I'll be able to... based on their experience in the session.

2. Extend the protocol with a role-alike or cross role sharing (e.g., grade level or vertical team) and a discussion of ways colleagues can support one another or what resources will be needed, etc.

Logistics

Materials and Preparation

Recording sheets with stems:

If I remember to...

Then I'll be able to...

PowerPoint® direction slides

Time

5–10 minutes

Grouping: 4–6

Variations

The If-Then can be focused on self-assessment of one's role in group development. Individuals generate a specific behavior or disposition that they want to be conscious of to produce a positive result for the group.

Use the individually generated If-Then items for a Give One to Get One protocol (see page 8).

Example

Topic: Skillful Facilitation

If I remember to...

stand still while giving directions

Then I'll be able to...

more effectively focus the attention of group members

Moving Forward

Logistics

Materials and Preparation

Create and duplicate a Moving Forward planning page with the skills to be assessed.

PowerPoint® direction slides

Time

10–15 Minutes

Grouping: Full group

Purpose

Moving Forward is a self-assessment and planning guide that supports participants in selecting learning strategies, opportunities for practice in daily work and application arenas for the skills being developed.

Intention

This strategy structures self-reflection and choice making in the adult learning process. Using this tool increases the likelihood that participants will practice and refine skills and apply them in work settings.

Tip

Use this tool at critical junctures with school improvement processes during which staff members are developing new instructional approaches and/or social skills initiatives with students. This is especially valuable when the innovation requires significant changes in habits or patterns for the adult learners such as using different language patterns when communicating with students.

Variation

Have partners consult with each other when they are developing practice and application ideas.

Instructions to Group Leader

1. Distribute the Moving Forward planning pages.
2. Ask participants to assess their own level of knowledge integration and application by using the following code:
   - N – new to me
   - K – knew about
   - A – apply when I remember
   - I – integrated into my practice
3. Have participants identify selected skills to isolate for practice and refinement. They also develop strategies for learning and refining the selected skills.
4. Participants then identify critical applications arenas for the selected skills.
5. Invite participants to share some of their learning goals, strategies and applications with their neighbors.

Example

Topic: Non-verbal Teaching Skills

Strategies Code: **N**= New to me **K** = Knew about **A**= Apply when I remember **I** = Integrated into my practice	Learning Goals • New learning • Applying & refining skills • Integrating skills	Practice Opportunities
1. Pause after asking questions to increase student think time <u>A</u> 2. Provide a summary paraphrase after 3-4 student responses	To integrate this skill so I apply it with unconscious competence	During social studies instruction
<u>N</u> 3. Provide specific feed back to students, rather than general praise <u>K</u>	To begin applying this skill on a consistent basis	Daily, with reading groups

Outcome Mapping

Purpose

Outcome Mapping is an effective way to focus a group's energy and attention away from wallowing in the details of some problem or issue and moving the focus toward developing positive outcomes for those same situations. It is a graphic backwards-planning technique that deconstructs a desired outcome into the underlying behaviors, skills and dispositions required to produce that result.

Intention

This graphic tool provides a focusing point for the planning process and shapes the thinking of group members.

The physical production of the graphic organizer creates a high level of interaction and allows group members to isolate and clarify the essential behaviors and interventions that might produce the intended outcome.

Logistics

Materials and Preparation

Three pieces of chart paper and colored markers

Divide charts into columns labeled 1–6 and post in reverse order.

PowerPoint® direction slides

Time

40–60 minutes

Grouping: 4–6 or full group

Instructions to Group Leader

1. Chart one: Identify a condition or problem for which the group will be generating an action plan. Note: The group may have previously identified the issue or topic.

2. Have group members briefly describe the problem. Record a short statement of the problem in the right hand column of the first chart (column 1).

3. Develop an outcome for the problem or issue. Record this in column 2. Be sure to state the outcome in the positive (what you want to have happen) and not in the negative (what you don't want to have happen).

4. Chart two: Generate specific things you would see and hear in products and performances required to produce the planned outcome. Record these in column 3. Tip: Generate 10–12 ideas then select the 3–4 most catalytic items that focus the rest of the plan. These items become important elements upon which to base any assessment and project-monitoring plan.

5. Reflecting on the desired behaviors in column 3, develop a list of the internal resources people will need to produce these desired behaviors including knowledge, skills and dispositions. Record these in column 4.

6. Chart three: This chart represents the support system for those who will be making the behavioral changes noted on the previous chart. In column 5 list the specific behaviors these growth agents will offer those making the change. These should include specific things you would hope to see and hear in products and performances generated by the growth agents.

7. Reflecting on the desired behaviors in column 5, develop a list of the internal resources growth agents will need to produce these desired behaviors including knowledge, skills and dispositions. Record these in column 6.

Tips

Caution the group against the temptation to tell stories and share too many examples while they are describing the problem or outcome.

Apply think-pair-share or round-robin patterns (see page 89) to balance participation and encourage full engagement by all group members.

Variations

For instructional change projects use an eight-column outcome map.

- Column 1: problem
- Column 2: outcome
- Column 3: desired student behaviors
- Column 4: internal resources students require to perform those behaviors
- Column 5: desired teaching behaviors
- Column 6: internal resources teachers require to perform those behaviors
- Column 7: desired teamwork behaviors
- Column 8: internal resources teams require to perform those behaviors.

Example

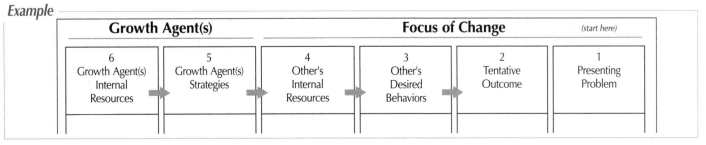

P+ M- I*

Logistics

Materials and Preparation

Create and duplicate P+ M- I* recording worksheets or use large chart paper and felt tip markers.

PowerPoint® direction slides

Time

15 minutes

Grouping: 4–6

Tips

Model the process; be sure participants understand that interesting is neither a plus nor a minus. For example, interesting points might include effects of the idea, or projections.

Offer a pass option during brainstorming process.

Remind groups that brainstorming is nonjudgmental. Explanations, qualifications or judgments distort the process and bog down the group work.

Variations

Offer a minute of think time for each group member to generate at least one idea in each category before beginning the brainstorming.

Have individuals record their own P+ M- I* ideas before the round-robin sharing.

Purpose

P+ M- I*, developed by Edward de Bono, structures examination and reflection on options under consideration. Given a topic, groups brainstorm the pros (pluses); cons (minuses) and interesting elements associated with the topic or idea. The interesting items include both gray areas that are neither positive nor negative as well as items that are unknowns or curiosities.

Intention

This strategy both honors and expands individual and group viewpoints by forcing group members to generate both pros and cons, no matter what their initial opinion might be. It promotes focus, energy and balanced participation, and is a low-risk method for exploring controversial or emotionally charged topics.

Instructions to Group Leader

1. Designate a recorder (or have groups choose one) and explain that the brainstorming for each category must remain exclusive to that category.
2. Direct groups to brainstorm pluses, using a Brainstorm and Pass pattern (see page 89).
3. After three minutes, have them repeat the process generating minuses.
4. After three minutes, have them repeat the process generating interesting points or ideas.
5. Finally, each table group shares their questions, and charts 1–2 for full group posting.

Example

Topic: Lengthening the School Day

P+	M-	I*
Opportunity to reinforce skills with struggling students	Students and teachers may be tired at end of day	Provide speakers/mentors from community to share with students
Can extend or add enrichment activities	Adds additional preparation for teachers	Have older students mentor younger students during extended time
Can use for advisory program	May impact bus schedules or family child care	Students can engage in project-based learning
		Teachers teach topic/unit that is their passion; students can choose as electives

Plan-a-Disaster

Purpose

Plan-a-Disaster is a planning tool for helping groups think through essential elements of what not to do if they want a plan to succeed. It can be used as an activating strategy at the beginning of a planning session to loosen up the group and get the process rolling. It can also be used later in a planning process to check assumptions and help the group anticipate implementation issues and nuances.

Intention

This strategy widens frames of reference by increasing awareness of potentially unanticipated outcomes of carrying out a plan or possible details that might be overlooked during implementation of an initiative. Plan-a-Disaster adds humor and energy to the work of planning groups.

Logistics

Materials and Preparation

Chart Paper

PowerPoint® direction slides

Time

Varies depending on the complexity of the plan being developed; generally 30–40 minutes

Grouping: 4–6

Instructions to Group Leader

Identify a goal that the group hopes to achieve.

1. With this goal in mind ask the group to define the opposite outcome in rich detail.

   What might they see if the negative outcomes were to happen?

   What might they hear if the negative outcomes were to happen?

   Where might they see and hear these indicators?

   Which constituencies or stakeholders might be most affected by the negative outcomes?

2. Select the critical attributes related to each of the questions above and develop detailed plans for achieving those outcomes.

   What essential steps in communicating and implementing the plan might need to occur to produce each negative attribute?

3. When the negative plans are fleshed out, asks the group to pause and reflect on the implications for the positive planning processes and implementation efforts in which they hope to engage.

Tips

Use this strategy as a scaffold to build confidence, readiness and positive working relationships when launching a new initiative or change effort.

Appoint a recorder and use chart paper to record the negative plan(s) as they emerge.

Once the essential negative attributes are defined, subdivide the group and assign each subgroup the task of developing the plan for that outcome.

Variation

Use the disaster plan to shape the criteria for assessing the effectiveness of the final positive plan the group produces.

Example

Issue: Developing a Strategic Plan

Ideal Goal: An effective and community supported five-year strategic plan

Undesired Negative Outcome: A boilerplate document that gets little notice and is not taken seriously by the staff or community

- No community support for budget and tax support

  To achieve this, be sure to limit public engagement and communication and be sure the district's website is boring and hard to navigate

- Staff resists any program changes

  To achieve this, do endless surveys with no follow-up

- Student achievement stagnates

  To achieve this, don't talk honestly with staff and parents about student learning issues and achievement gaps

- Staff recruiting becomes difficult

  To achieve this, don't let the human resources department know about district goals, successful programs and professional development opportunities that the district provides to staff members

- Area realtors badmouth the district

  To achieve this, don't work with the local press to tell the positive stories about the district and don't send press releases to realtors

Pluses and Wishes

Logistics

Materials and Preparation

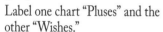

Two to four chart stands

Markers

Sticky notes

Position 2–4 chart stands, depicting on group size, in front of the room – in full view of the whole group.

Label one chart "Pluses" and the other "Wishes."

If using the "Gots and Wants" variation, distribute a stack of sticky notes to each table group.

PowerPoint® direction slides

Time

5–10 minutes

Grouping: 4–6

Tip

If needed, clarify specific wishes to check for the degree to which these items are important to other group members or are unique to individual preferences.

Variations

"Gots and Wants." Distribute sticky notes to each table group and ask group members to list on separate notes specific things that they "Got" from the content and processes. Using additional sticky notes have table groups list things they "Want" in the content and processes during future session.

Label a chart "Gots" and another chart "Wants." Have group members post their sticky notes on the appropriate chart.

Place charts at the door and use the sticky notes as exit slips as participants leave the session.

Purpose

Pluses and Wishes is an efficient method for eliciting feedback from a group. This is especially important when working with the same group over time. The pluses represent the positive ideas from the content and ways of working during the session that supported engagement and learning for individuals and the group as a whole. The wishes represent ideas and ways of working that group members would like more of, less of or modified in some way in upcoming sessions.

Intention

This strategy gives individual group members and the group as a whole a shared means for reflecting on their experience and proposing modifications for future sessions. The Pluses and Wishes tool provides group members with an opportunity to share their perspectives on the content and processes and to compare those with the perceptions and learning needs of others in the group. This strategy also offers insights to group leaders that might influence modifications to the design of upcoming sessions.

Instructions to Group Leader

1. Have group members reflect on their experiences and consider Pluses and Wishes related to the content and processes.

2. Recruit a recorder.

3. First elicit Pluses from group members. Paraphrase responses to clarify the intention and to compress language to chart-length phrases to record on the chart.

4. Then elicit Wishes from group members for things that they want more of, less of or would rather have structured differently in future sessions. Again, paraphrase and compress the response and record these on the Wishes Chart.

Spend-a-Buck

Purpose

Spend-a-Buck is an assessment tool that helps individuals and groups determine relative priorities within a list of options, interests or actions. Each group member is offered an imaginary stack of 100 pennies for distribution across the items of choice.

Intention

This strategy promotes choice making and personalization. It allows individuals to reflect on their own preferences, strengths and interests. Spend-a-Buck also supports group members in appreciating the variety of interests and perspectives of others. This tool is a useful self-assessment at a midpoint in a project or learning series.

Instructions to Group Leader

1. Display a slide or chart that presents the options, actions or interest areas of choice. Distribute recording sheets listing the options.

2. Describe the Spend-a-Buck procedure: Participants may "stack" as many or as few of their "pennies" next to each option as they desire. The goal is to create as clear a representation as possible of their personal interests.

3. Form task groups or learning groups by having people join others with similar interests.

   Note: Group members without strong preferences or needs can then balance out the numbers in the subgroups.

Logistics

Materials and Preparation

Recording sheet with options listed (if known ahead of time)

Chart paper for master list

PowerPoint® direction slides

Time

10–15 minutes depending on group size.

Grouping: Full group

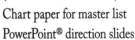

Tips

Spend-a-Buck works best when the number of options is limited, typically 3–5 choices.

This tool stacks well with Go To Your Corners (see page 9).

This tool is a useful self-assessment at a midpoint in a project or learning series.

Variations

Give participants 100 sticky dots each to place on a public chart. This is especially important when group members need to see the relative support for options and proposed actions.

With a calculator in hand, have each group member report the number of pennies they placed next to each item. Add these together and record the group's total for each item on a public chart. This is especially useful if the group is using Spend-a-Buck as a decision making tool.

Example

Topic: Study Group Options

• Differentiated learning	33
• Technology integration	24
• Reading in the content areas	21
• Formative assessment	22
	——
	100

T-Charts

Logistics

Materials and Preparation

Recording sheets with two columns or blank note paper

PowerPoint® direction slides

Time

15–20 minutes

Grouping: 2–6

Purpose

T-Charts is a flexible and time efficient tool. Juxtaposing two ways of thinking about a topic or event offers groups and group members a way to explore tough-to-talk-about elements regarding arenas of professional practice.

Intention

This reflective strategy is an efficient way to begin a plan of action or a commitment to applying new practices. It provides some individual think time as well as a structure to focus sharing.

Tip

Group members can complete their T-chart recording sheet on their own and bring it to the session.

Variations

Use the T-chart format electronically and share online.

Use the completed T-chart recording sheet to focus one-to-one or small group planning conversations.

Instructions to Group Leader

1. Ask participants to work individually first, completing their recording sheet by filling in each column with several ideas.

2. After a designated amount of time, structure interaction or full group exploration of the individual responses.

3. It is particularly effective to structure a conversation that focuses on similarities and differences between individual assessments.

Example

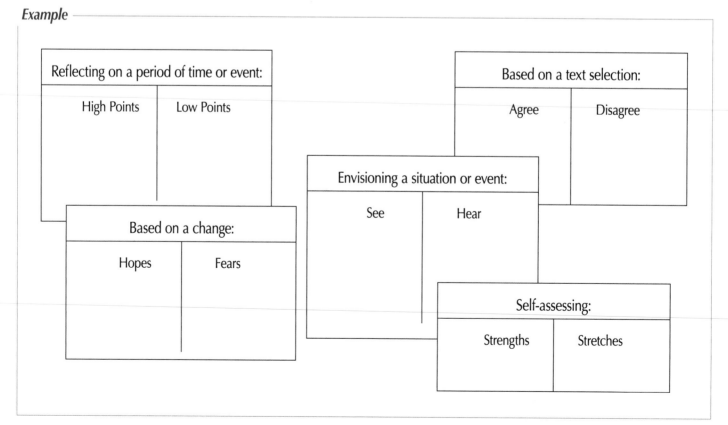

Reflecting on a period of time or event:

| High Points | Low Points |

Based on a text selection:

| Agree | Disagree |

Envisioning a situation or event:

| See | Hear |

Based on a change:

| Hopes | Fears |

Self-assessing:

| Strengths | Stretches |

The Matrix

Purpose

The Matrix vividly displays data generated by a group as a cluster diagram, creating a focal point for dialogue and discussion. The data represents group members' self-assessment about skill level, interest, commitment or belief related to an issue, problem or change initiative.

Intention

By functioning as a focusing point, the matrix creates a psychologically safe way for a group to explore perceived skills or readiness related to a topic or change initiative. It offers a snapshot of the group that serves to depersonalize the data, so the conversation can focus on exploring issues and potential next steps. This strategy creates shared understanding of others' perspectives and a greater readiness for collaborative action planning.

Logistics

Materials and Preparation

Large display with a gridded matrix using a scale of 0–10 on each axis (see below). Create a recording sheet for participant self-assessment or use blank notepaper.

Small sticky dots (one per participant)

PowerPoint® direction slides

Time

25–30 minutes

Grouping: 4–6

Instructions to Group Leader

1. Create task groups of 4–6, providing each participant with a sticky dot and a recording sheet or blank notepaper for recording their self-assessment.

2. Given the matrix display, ask participants to rate themselves on each axis.

3. After 3–5 minutes (to complete the individual rating), have participants go to the prepared wall display and place their sticky dot in the appropriate spot, forming a cluster graph.

4. When all responses have been posted and the graph is complete, organize a group exploration of the data (see sample facilitator questions below).

Tips

This strategy works best with groups larger than 20.

It is particularly effective to organize task groups of mixed roles and/or experience to enrich the discussion.

Variations

Insert a predicting stage before participants post their responses. Ask table group members to predict, and record what the graph might look like and some reasons why they are making this prediction. Provide a blank recording sheet for this step, so groups can record both their predictions and assumptions.

Use different color dots for different role groups (e.g., blue for all elementary teachers, red for middle school, green for high school, etc.).

Example

Topic: Data-driven Dialogue

Facilitator Questions

What strikes you as you observe the data?

What are some patterns emerging from the graph?

What surprises you?

What are some inferences related to the data; the group; the topic?

What conclusions might you draw?

How do the data help inform potential next steps?

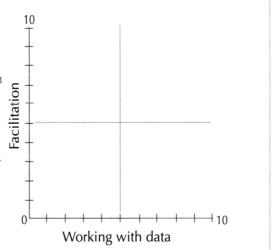

1. Individually rate your level of knowledge, skill and confidence in facilitating data-driven dialogue using a scale of 0-10.

2. Individually rate your level of knowledge, skill and confidence in working with data using a scale of 0-10.

3. Place a dot at the appropriate intersection on the graph.

Traffic Light

Logistics

Materials and Preparation

Recording sheets with a "traffic light" or space for recording commitments to actions

Red Light = stop
Yellow Light = continue
Green Light = begin

PowerPoint® direction slides

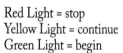

Time

15–20 minutes

Grouping: 2–6

Tips

This strategy is particularly effective with grade level, department or implementation teams.

If time is short, limit completion to "Red Light" and "Green Light" actions.

Variations

Use the traffic light format electronically and share online.

Ask individual group members to complete their traffic light after a work session, and bring it to the next meeting to share and compare with others.

Purpose

Traffic Light uses the convention of a traffic signal to organize each group member's reflections, in preparation for individual or shared action.

Intention

This reflective strategy is an efficient way to begin a plan of action or a commitment to applying new practices. It provides individual think time, as well as a structure to focus sharing.

Instructions to Group Leader

1. Create work groups (pairs or larger) and provide a recording sheet for each group.

2. Ask group members to work individually first, completing their recording sheet with commitments to actions that will:

   Red Light – stop
   Yellow Light – continue
   Green Light – begin

   based on the work or training session.

3. After a designated amount of time, structure small or full group interaction exploration of the individual commitments.

Example

Topic: Productive Meetings

Based on your learning in this session, what might you:

- **Stop doing**

Working without goals for us as a group
Telling elaborate stories that use up meeting time
Asking for detailed explanations based on personal concerns

- **Continue doing**

Developing clear agendas with specified starting and ending times
Sharing the role of the facilitator
Using chart paper for public recording

- **Start doing**

Using explicit strategies and protocols to guide our work
Preserving time at the end of the meeting to reflect on how we're doing
Setting goals to ensure growth as a group

Unpacking

Purpose

The **Unpacking** strategy structures reflection of participants' experiences in preparation for sharing. It provides an opportunity for self-assessment and a way to explore others' experiences for similarities and differences, and to surface questions about the application of a new initiative or the development of a skill set.

Intention

This strategy balances participation, expands the individual and shared knowledge base, and increases confidence in applying new methods or skills. The individual reflection step gives participants an opportunity to assess their experiences.

Logistics

Materials and Preparation

Create and duplicate recording sheets to structure individual reflections with columns labeled "Success," "Challenges," and "Questions."

PowerPoint® direction slides

Time

25–30 minutes

Grouping: 4–6

Instructions to Group Leader

1. Direct individuals to complete their Unpacking recording sheet. Note: This step can be done outside of the meeting setting.
2. After 4–5 minutes choose a recorder and initiate table group sharing using a round-robin protocol (see page 89), focusing on Successes only and listening and recording themes.
3. Ask each table group to share a theme or statement about its successes.
4. Repeat the process for Challenges.
5. Finally, each table group shares their Questions and charts 1 or 2 examples for full group posting.

Tips

Groups will need to record their Successes and Challenges while sharing.

Alert groups to avoid story-telling, excessive anecdotal detail or background information when sharing successes and challenges.

Remind groups that the intention is not to solve colleague's challenges, but simply to name them.

Example

Topic: Implementing a Student Advisement Program

What's in your luggage?

- **Successes**

Positive student response
Students showing up on time
Stronger relationships with students

- **Challenges**

Time pressure
Trust levels between students
Navigating the line between appropriate support and providing therapy

- **Questions**

How will this program influence student learning over time?
What additional skills and training might teachers need to increase their confidence?
How will students respond in the 2nd and 3rd years of the program as they get
    additional experience with the advisement process and protocols?

Windows and Mirrors

Logistics

Materials and Preparation

T-chart recording sheet or chart paper and felt tip markers

PowerPoint® direction slides

Time

20–30 minutes

Grouping: 4–6

Purpose

Windows and Mirrors provides a psychologically safe way for a group to gain insights into their own process and relationship skills. This strategy uses visualization to enable group members to take an outside, or third person, perspective, describing what they might see through a window or reflected in a mirror.

Intention

This strategy increases group members' consciousness about how individual decisions, choices and behaviors influence group work. It also provides a protocol for developing criteria for group work or any task.

Tips

Monitor group work to be sure that they generate specific, observable behaviors.

It may be useful to create a master list of the task groups' reports.

Instructions to Group Leader

1. Determine a recorder for each task group.

2. Ask task groups to imagine that they are viewing a particular scenario through a special one-way window, and to describe what they are seeing and hearing. Groups should list these observations on the See/Hear T-chart. For example, ask groups to imagine they are observing a group struggling with data work or a classroom that is out of control.

3. Ask recorders to share some of the items on their charts with the full group.

4. Now ask groups to imagine that they are in a special room in which they can observe their own behavior reflected in mirrored walls. For example, ask group members to imagine they are the leader of the group described above, or the teacher in that classroom. Ask task groups to generate specific things that they might see and hear themselves doing to make a difference (e.g., increase the data group's focus and productivity or increase management and learning in the classroom).

Example

Topic: Group Development

WINDOW		MIRROR	
See	**Hear**	**See**	**Hear**
Grading papers	Side talk	Eyes focused on one speaker at a time	Paraphrasing
Texting	Excuses	Head nods	Open-ended questions
Working on laptop	One person dominating conversation	Public charting for group memory	Checking for understanding of colleagues ideas
Eyes down or arms crossed	Defensive or accusatory tones	Smiles or thoughtful expressions	Clarifying process to ensure balance of participation of all group members
Frowns, bored looks			Silence - pausing to think

Strategies for Dialogue and Discussion

Meaningful group work relies on the engaged minds and hearts of all members. Strategies for including all voices, listening to others and being listened to by others develop mutual respect and balance a willingness to entertain new ideas with the passion for expressing one's own. Skillful dialogue and discussion are essential group processes that produce these results. Each process has a distinct purpose and both are important modes of discourse.

Dialogue is a reflective learning process in which group members seek to understand one another's viewpoints and deeply held assumptions. In dialogue the goal is shared understanding, not agreement.

Discussion focuses on the parts and their relationships. Discussion involves analysis of ideas, cause-effect, part to whole, comparing and contrasting key elements, and anticipating the effects of proposed actions. In discussion the goal is agreement on the distinctions between and implications of possible courses of action.

Strategies that structure dialogue and discussion uncover assumptions, making them available for exploration and analysis. They become vehicles for investigating multiple perspectives, ideas and orientations. These protocols provide external guidelines that allow groups to engage with tough-to-talk-about topics in safe and productive ways.

Dialogue disintegrates when group members misunderstand the intention and seek to persuade others of the merits of their viewpoint or ideas. Discussion breaks down when judgment and debate replace thoughtful listening and skilled advocacy.

The strategies that follow illuminate the intention of each mode of discourse and support effective engagement. These strategies are especially necessary when topics are hot, tempers are high and time is tight.

NOTE: Strategies for engaging in dialogue or discussion are more effective when stacked with other functions. For example, a full process agenda might include an activating strategy, a text processing strategy, a strategy for dialogue and, finally, a summarizing strategy.

Artifact Hunt

Logistics

Materials and Preparation

Chart paper

Felt tip markers

Artifacts (provided by participants)

PowerPoint® direction slides

Time

45–60 minutes

Grouping: 4–5

Purpose

Artifact Hunt is an anthropological quest to better understand the culture that surrounds an issue, a group or a plan. This tool offers a reality check for plans, projects and teamwork by offering a glimpse into the current cultural context. It also provides a structure for envisioning the cultural elements necessary for success.

Intention

This strategy focuses attention on the existing organizational or group culture and provides a low-risk, high-engagement way to assess the values and beliefs it reflects. It also offers a way to check for congruence between the value base of a proposed initiative and the environment in which it is going to be implemented, offering a way to envision and plan for any necessary cultural shifts.

Tips

Provide clear examples of values and beliefs that might be reflected in specific artifacts.

Alert groups to self-monitor for excessive anecdotes related to their artifacts that might bog down group work.

Variation

Use this process to assess group development. Direct the group members to apply the process to their own group work.

Instructions to Group Leader

1. Prior to the scheduled meeting, ask group members to collect and bring (or at least list) artifacts that they might show to a visitor to help explain what is valued in their organization or group. Examples might include awards, schedules, photographs, memos or objects.

2. In task groups of 4–5, have groups share and categorize their collections.

3. After 15–20 minutes, groups transfer the category labels on to blank wall charts.

4. For each category, the group records the values and beliefs that the articles within the category represent. These might be both positive and negative.

5. After 15–20 minutes, each task group selects an artifact(s) that exemplifies meaningful values in the existing culture and share this with the larger group.

6. Referencing the project, plan or issue being considered, have small groups identify three or four core values within the existing culture they will need to address in order to achieve success. Note: The values identified have either a positive or negative impact on the issue.

7. After 15–20 minutes, focus the full group on a specific date in the future. Invite them to envision the artifacts they might find that would indicate successful implementation or solution.

Example

Topic: Examining a School's Culture

Artifacts:	Values:
Daily Schedule	Order and Predictability
Minutes from Staff Meetings	Hierarchy and Status
Pictures of Posters on the Walls	Tradition
Photos of the Staff Room and its Bulletin Boards	
Yearbooks	
School Awards	
Photos of Trophy Cases	
Student Newspapers	
Transcripts of Daily P.A. Announcements	

Card Stack and Shuffle

Purpose

Card Stack and Shuffle provides a structured process for surfacing the assumptions and beliefs that underlie and often constrain group members' thinking.

Intention

This strategy offers a low-risk method for surfacing and exploring assumptions. Although assumptions influence thinking, they often remain unexamined. The interaction follows individual generation of assumptions, provides think time and increases balance and inclusion of all group members.

Logistics

Materials and Preparation

A stack of index cards for each table, at least 2–3 cards for each participant

PowerPoint® direction slides

Time

15–20 minutes

Grouping: 4–6

Instructions to Group Leader

1. Direct participants to distribute blank index cards evenly among the table group members.

2. Individually, participants create a stack of cards that relate to the topic under discussion by completing a stem such as "The most important method for assessing student learning is…" A stem completion offers a useful scaffold for generating personal perspectives and still reveals assumptions for group exploration.

3. Emphasize that there should be only one response per card.

4. After 4–5 minutes of writing time, have group members stack their cards in the center of the table and shuffle the pile. Note: When working with multiple groups, pass the card stack so no table group is working with its own cards.

5. In turn, each group member chooses a card and reads it aloud to the table group. Members explore the item and generate and record possible assumptions for the idea on that card.

6. Group members then examine their list of assumptions and select 2–3 that might have the greatest implications for their work. They then record these on the left side of a T-chart.

7. On the right side of the T-chart the group then records the implications of these driving assumptions.

8. The implications become the jumping off point for an action planning process.

Tip

Model several examples before participants work on their own.

Variations

Use two stems that tease out contrasts or distinctions about the topic, such as

Successful learners…; struggling learners….

Effective writing teachers…; successful student writers….

Example

Topic: Effective Classroom Management

Stem Completion: Effective classroom management includes *clear routines and procedures.*

Assumptions	Implications
CR management requires structure Teachers need to teach routines to students Routines should be developmentally appropriate	Teachers need a repertoire of effective structures

Compass Points

Logistics

Materials and Preparation

Chart paper placed at four points in the room

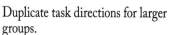

Each chart labeled with the points on a compass (North, East, South, West)

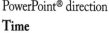

Duplicate task directions for larger groups.

PowerPoint® direction slides

Time

20–30 minutes depending on group size

Grouping: Individual, task groups and full group

Purpose

Compass Points is an energizing way to introduce the topic of personal working style preferences for individuals within task groups. Individuals select a personal point of preference and form clusters at charts located at that directional indicator in the room. These working clusters then chart their responses to three prompts for sharing with the larger group.

Adapted from *turningpoints.org*

Intention

This strategy uses physical movement, public charting and elements of group-generated humor to surface and explore the variety of working style preferences in groups. In the process, the tensions between group members that arise from these preferences emerge. By making them public these tensions become normalized and depersonalized.

Tips

Keep the chart production time tight to limit the possibility of storytelling and elaboration by the group members.

Sequence the full group sharing by having all compass point groups first share their strengths, then share their limitations and finally share what others need to know about them.

Emphasize that the term preference is used to indicate that we all can flex to work with others who are not wired like us.

Variations

As an additional step after the chart generation and sharing process, have individuals select the style that they find most difficult to work with. Individuals then move to that compass point, cluster and explore ways in which they might need to flex against their own preferences to work productively with others who have that working style. If time allows, invite participants to share some of their thinking about flexing to work across style preferences.

Instructions to Group Leader

1. Project a slide with the four compass points and their descriptors.

    North: Just get it done – like to act – try things out

    East: Look at the big picture – speculate – consider ideas

    South: Consider everyone's feelings – to hear and honor all voices

    West: Pay attention to details – like to know who, what, where and how before acting

2. Give individuals a moment to identify their personal compass point. Caution participants that while this is a bit oversimplified they need to select one of the four and not some midpoint between any two.

3. Direct individuals to cluster at the selected compass points and form groups of 4–6 to produce a chart by responding to the following three prompts.

    • List four strengths of your style preference

    • List four limitations of your style preference

    • List some examples of what others need to know about people with your style preference to make your work together more productive and successful.

4. Have people at each compass point share key points from their charts with the full group.

Example

Personal Style

North	Just get it done	Like to act, try things out, plunge in
East	Look at the big picture	Like to speculate, consider possibilities before acting
South	Consider everyone's feelings	Like to hear and honor all voices before acting
West	Pay attention to the details	Like to know who, what, where, how before acting

Conflict Conversation Template

Purpose

The Conflict Conversation Template is a dialogue tool for exploring conflicts within or between groups. It is especially useful for engaging groups in addressing persistent and recurring patterns that produce undesired outcomes for the group or others with whom group members interact. This structure offers specific prompts to guide the group in its dialogue about emotionally charged issues.

Adapted from *Garmston and Wellman, 2009.*

Intention

This strategy widens perspectives by providing a psychologically safe environment for examining tough-to-talk-about topics. It helps group members frame more positive outcomes by helping them to develop more global perspectives on an issue.

Instructions to Group Leader

1. Identify a conflict that exists within the group or between this group and others.
2. Pose the prompts on a slide or chart and reveal in four clusters (1&2, 3–5, 6&7, 8&9) to provide time for thinking. Have group members record their responses on index cards, one card for each prompt.
3. Using a round-robin pattern (see page 89), have group members share their responses. Each round should focus on one prompt cluster in turn. Encourage group members to paraphrase one another as they share to find common ground and clarify differences.
4. Have pairs or trios craft summaries of the dialogue and share those with their table group.

Logistics

Materials and Preparation

Nine blank index cards per participant

Chart or slide with question prompts for the dialogue

PowerPoint® direction slides

Time

30–40 minutes

Grouping: 4–6

Tips

Offering the dialogue prompts in clusters encourages richer exploration of each question at both the writing and sharing stage.

When the conflict involves multiple groups, run the process with each group separately.

Variation

Have a different group member facilitate each dialogue prompt. Encourage the facilitator to paraphrase, summarize and organize the thinking of group members and then probe for clarification and elaboration of ideas.

Example

Dialogue Prompts:

1. What is your relationship to this conflict?
2. How do you feel about this conflict?

3. What are the best possible outcomes of this conflict?
4. What are the worst possible outcomes of this conflict?
5. What are the worst possible outcomes for not addressing this conflict?

6. What do you think the best possible outcomes for this conflict are for the other party?
7. What do you think the worst possible outcomes for this conflict are for the other party?

8. What are you willing to do to achieve the best possible outcome?
9. What would you like the other party to do to achieve the best possible outcome?

Consensogram

Logistics

Materials and Preparation

Three to five Consensogram questions to which participants can respond on a 0–100 scale

Recording sheets with Consensogram questions and a rating scale

Large charts with Consensogram questions posted on top and a rating scale on the bottom

Small sticky notes or dots (one per question times the number of participants)

PowerPoint® direction slides

Time

25–30 minutes

Grouping: 4–6

Tips

The most effective questions surface dynamics or tensions related to the questions and the overall topic. For this reason, questions that juxtapose perspectives, such as self versus others, immediate versus long term and interest versus knowledge or skill will create the dynamics necessary for productive dialogue.

This strategy works best with groups larger than 20. It is particularly effective to organize task groups of mixed roles and/or experience.

Variations

Insert a predicting stage before participants post their responses. Ask table group members to predict and record what the bar graphs might look like and some reasons why they are making this prediction. Provide a blank worksheet for this step, so groups can record both their predictions and assumptions.

Use different color sticky notes for different role groups (e.g., blue for building administrators, red for teachers, green for central office, etc.).

Sample Facilitator Questions:

What strikes you as you observe these data?
What are some patterns emerging from the charts?
What surprises you?
What conclusions might you draw?
What are some inferences related to the data, the group, the topic?
How do these data help inform potential next steps?

Purpose

Consensogram vividly displays data generated by a group as bar graphs, creating a focal point for dialogue. The data represents group members' perceptions of skill level, interest, commitment or belief related to an issue, problem or change initiative.

Intention

By functioning as a focusing point, the Consensogram creates a psychologically safe way to explore deep-seated beliefs, values and assumptions. It honors individual viewpoints while increasing understanding, or at least awareness, of others' perspectives. It is especially useful for surfacing outlier perspectives that appear distinctly different from the mainstream responses.

Instructions to Group Leader

1. Create task groups of 4–6, providing each participant with sticky notes or dots for each question to be explored and a worksheet listing the Consensogram questions with the rating scale (0–100) for each.

2. Display the questions for consideration on a chart or screen and direct participants to individually respond to each question, based on their own perceptions, using the scale of 0–100. Note: Responses must be in increments of 10, with no negative numbers.

3. After 4–5 minutes (to complete the individual scaling), have participants transfer their response to each question to a sticky note or color dot.

4. Have participants go to the prepared wall charts and place their sticky note or dot in the appropriate columns, forming bar graphs.

5. When all responses have been posted and the graphs are complete, organize a group exploration of the data (see sample facilitator questions below).

6. Groups review the information on their original chart and prepare any questions that might occur to them.

Example

Consensogram

Please respond to the following on a scale from 0 to 100 in increments of 10.

1. To what degree do you believe that building a collaborative learning team affects student learning?
   0 10 20 30 40 50 60 70 80 90 100

2. To what degree do you believe the Administrative Council is a collaborative learning team?
   0 10 20 30 40 50 60 70 80 90 100

3. To what extent are you personally committed to this goal? (intentionally monitor your actions, apply linguistic skills, etc.)
   0 10 20 30 40 50 60 70 80 90 100

4. To what extent do you believe others are committed to this goal? (intentionally monitor their actions, apply linguistic skills, etc.)
   0 10 20 30 40 50 60 70 80 90 100

Consensogram

1. To what degree do you believe that building a collaborative learning team affects student learning?

   0 10 20 30 40 50 60 70 80 90 100

Topic: Collaborative Learning Teams

Consensus Clusters

Purpose

Consensus Clusters is an idea generation pattern with several variations that build consensus for proposals and decisions. Individuals first clarify and record their own suggested actions and reasoning related to a specific topic or proposal and then move to paired interactions to exchange ideas and clarify thinking. Pairs then group into larger configurations to extend the sharing and clarifying process. Finally, the whole group convenes to examine and refine emerging proposals.

Intention

This strategy gradually widens the perspective from the individual to the larger group so that all voices find a place in the conversation and a stake in the outcome.

Logistics

Materials and Preparation

Index cards

Chart paper and markers

Public timer

PowerPoint® direction slides

Time

60–90 minutes

Grouping: Pairs, task groups, full group

Instructions to Group Leader

1. Ask each group member to advocate for specific actions related to a topic before the group and record his or her thinking on an index card. These advocacies should be related to choice points or decisions for shaping the direction of the group such as problems to work on together, desired courses of action based on previous work or other arenas where the group or organization might need to focus its energy and resources.

2. After the designated writing time, form pairs and invite partners to share their thinking with each other and to explore the assumptions and implications of their respective proposals.

3. After the designated paired time, form quartets or larger task groups to extend the sharing and inquiry process. Encourage the groups to listen carefully for common ground within their respective ideas.

4. Each group selects and records an agreed on advocacy on a sheet of chart paper for presentation to the full group.

5. Post the chart papers on a blank wall and arrange chairs in a semicircle pattern so that each participant has a clear sightline to the charts.

6. Request a period of silence so that everyone in the room has a chance to read the charted ideas.

7. After the designated reading time, open a space for participants to ask questions to clarify any ambiguous items. The authors of those ideas respond.

8. Regroup the charts to link related or overlapping proposals.

9. Examine the clusters and facilitate a feasibility conversation about how many of the proposed actions are possible to address given time, energy and resources. With this number in mind ask the group to prioritize the action items.

10. Select a subcommittee to refine the action steps for the selected items.

Tips

Use a public timer to manage the flow of each step and protect the overall time for completing the full process.

Use an organized group strategy to purposefully form the initial pairs. One choice point depending on the options before the group and the need for perspective is job-alike versus job-diverse pairs.

This process is most effective with groups that have some experience/skill in verbal and non-verbal communication patterns.

For task groups of 6 or more, designating one person to facilitate and manage time balances participation and better synchronizes the timing so that each working group is ready at the same time to move to the full group stage.

Variations

Use a 1–2–4 pattern* to work up to task groups to manage time efficiently.

Use a 1–2–4–8 pattern* to work up to task groups within a larger group to more slowly widen the frame.

Use a 1–2–6* pattern to work up to task groups with a group that has reasonable inquiry skills and patience with processes like this.

*grouping patterns

First Turn/Last Turn

Logistics

Materials and Preparation

Duplicate an appropriate text selection for each group member.

Highlight pens

PowerPoint® direction slides

Time

20–30 minutes

Grouping: 4–6

Purpose

First Turn/Last Turn is a highly structured protocol for organizing dialogue and collaborative inquiry. It is particularly effective for newly formed groups, or for any groups working with controversial or emotionally charged topics.

Intention

This strategy develops an appreciation for the power of listening and the personal and shared learning potential when exploring diverse perspectives. It develops deeper understandings for each group member; about themselves, their colleagues and the material being addressed.

Tips

Have group members read and highlight the selection on their own before the group session.

Give groups an opportunity to check for understanding of the protocol before designating an initiator.

Be sure each initiator gives group members an opportunity to find the identified section and scan it before moving to the round-robin.

Monitor group dynamics, gently intervening if cross-talk occurs.

Variation

Use this protocol with other focusing materials such as data, student work products, rubrics or lesson plans.

Instructions to Group Leader

1. Ask individuals to read the text selection and highlight 2–3 items that catch their attention.

   Note: This step can be done prior to the meeting.

2. Model the protocol, emphasizing the round-robin pattern (see page 89) with no cross-talk.

3. Determine who will initiate the process (be the first speaker). You can designate or the group can choose. The initiator takes the First Turn, sharing a highlighted item, but does not elaborate.

4. Moving to the right, each group member comments on the designated item, whether s/he highlighted it or not.

5. Finally, the rotation returns to the initiator, who gets the Last Turn, sharing his or her thinking about the highlighted item.

6. The process continues, moving to the right, with a new initiator.

In and Out of the Frame

Purpose

In and Out of the Frame is a tool for identifying and exploring the frames of reference that group members and others outside the group may be holding related to a topic under consideration. It is especially useful for planning groups that need to consider the viewpoints of others and communicate skillfully with those varied constituencies.

Intention

This simple graphic organizer structures exploration and synthesis of information, while incorporating and honoring individual points of view. The physical production of the graphic organizer creates a high level of interaction and a visual focusing point for sharing perspectives and clarifying understandings. This tool allows group members to see what is in their own frame of reference and supports them in stepping outside those frames to consider other perspectives.

Logistics

Materials and Preparation

Chart paper and a colored marker for each group

PowerPoint® direction slides

Time

30–40 minutes

Grouping: 4–6

Instructions to Group Leader

1. Form working groups and provision them with a sheet of chart paper and a marker.

2. Have a recorder draw a large rectangle on the chart paper to represent the frame.

3. Group members then brainstorm words and short phrases that they associate with the selected topic and record inside the frame.

4. After an appropriate period of brainstorming (8–10 minutes) have the groups categorize their items, using the top portion of their chart papers to list the category labels.

5. Assign each group another frame of reference as a lens through which to examine its chart, based on other perspectives that might need to be considered such as parents, students, community members, etc.

6. With a new pen color, groups should circle ideas inside the frame that people with their assigned perspective might also have included.

7. Ask groups to add ideas outside the frame on the bottom portion of the chart that people with their assigned perspective might have included that the group did not.

Tips

Remind groups that brainstorming is rapid generation of ideas with no elaboration or judgment.

When other items have been identified at the completion of Step 7, have groups identify those that might be most important to that constituency.

Variations

Have groups take a walking tour to view other groups' charts at the completion of Step 4. Invite them to add ideas to their own charts that they think might enrich their work.

For groups that have used this strategy previously, assign a specific frame of reference at the start of the activity and have different groups generate and categorize ideas from that perspective. Then post the charts and have the larger group explore the similarities and differences in the perspectives.

Example

Topic: Implementing Standards-based Grading

Connection to Standards	Outcomes	Impacts on/for Teaching	Impacts on Students
Perspectives Students Beyond just seat time May require more work How will it affect my GPA	Aligns work products to state standards Authentic demonstration of knowledge May be a new way of thinking about criteria for quality work Challenging Exciting Supports self-directedness Need PD to do well Will require collaboration and transparency		Perspectives Parents Why change May be unfair to students Teachers will need more skills My child may not do as well

Inter-VENN-tion

Logistics

Materials and Preparation

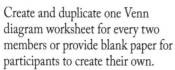

Determine categories for consideration for inside the "me-map."

Create and duplicate one "me-map" recording sheet for each group member.

Create and duplicate one Venn diagram worksheet for every two members or provide blank paper for participants to create their own.

PowerPoint® direction slides

Time

25–30 minutes

Grouping: Pairs, quartets

Tips

It is useful to model the process, especially at the initial stage.

Alert partners to Step 6, the cross introductions, so they can prepare.

To preserve meeting time, the individual "me-maps" can be completed prior to the meeting.

Variations

Use this protocol for participants to reflect on their growth as a group.

Use this protocol after input or exploration of information. For example, at the end of a workshop on formative assessment, put topics in the "me-map" like "things I remember," "important ideas," and "specific examples."

Purpose

Inter-VENN-tion is a flexible multistep strategy that structures an exchange and exploration of information that is individually and collectively relevant to the group members and to the topic at hand. It can be applied to a wide range of topics, including information about group members' interests and experiences. It can be applied to explore a topic while developing a school improvement plan, before launching an initiative, during implementation or as a reflective strategy afterwards.

Intention

This strategy is effective for building relationships as groups are forming. It is also effective for finding commonalities and distinctions between individual group member's experiences, perspectives, and knowledge about a topic under consideration.

Instructions to Group Leader

1. Display a "me-map" with topics/categories to be addressed, or ask group members to draw a circle on a blank piece of paper.

2. Direct group members to work individually to fill-in words/short phrases for each category displayed.

3. Once these "me-maps" are completed, organize partners.

4. Using the Venn recording sheet, or creating one, partners compare and contrast their individual thinking, placing the information in the appropriate space on the diagram. Encourage group members to add new information as it emerges during their exploration.

5. After 15–20 minutes connect sets of partners to create quartets (pairs squared).

6. Partners introduce each other and share a little bit about their conversation.

Example

Topic: Formative Assessment

self-assessment inventories

time required

teacher observations

student ownership of learning

learning logs

developing and choosing appropriate formative assessment tools

positive influence on instruction

Interview Carousel

Purpose

Interview Carousel is a versatile structure for deep exploration of ideas, experiences and reflections about a topic. Creating interview partners with a single question keeps the exchanges balanced and efficient.

Intention

This strategy expands the shared knowledge base regarding any project, initiative or body of information. It honors and allows time for the expression of individual viewpoints. The theme clusters at the final step give the group a chance to step back and "see" itself and its experiences from a wider perspective.

Instructions to Group Leader

1. Form groups of 4 and number off 1–4.
2. Provide each group member with the question page that corresponds with his or her number.
3. Direct group members to write a response to their own question in the first space.
4. After 3–5 minutes, establish interview partners: 1's and 2's; 3's and 4's. Partners interview each other and record responses on their own question sheet.
5. After approximately 8–10 minutes (4–5 minutes for each interview); switch partners (2's & 3's; 1's & 4's).
6. Continue the process until everyone has responded to all four questions.
7. Create like-number question groups (all the 1's, 2's, etc.). These groups share their collected responses and chart themes, patterns and significant ideas gleaned from the interviews.

Logistics

Materials and Preparation

Prepare four questions and create a question sheet for each one, with four spaces for written responses.

Number and print each question on its own page.

Chart paper for theme groups

PowerPoint® direction slides

Time

30–45 minutes

Grouping: Quartets

Tips

It is important to number the question pages (question 1, 2, 3, etc.). It is helpful to use a different color paper for each question.

Emphasize that this is an interview protocol; not a paired discussion. The interviewer should listen, periodically paraphrase and record.

Use a round-robin pattern (see page 89) for sharing in theme groups to balance participation.

Variations

Conduct a walk-about (see page 90) after theme groups have charted their work.

Engage groups in exploring the assumptions related to the themes and large ideas.

Example

Topic: Professional Learning Communities

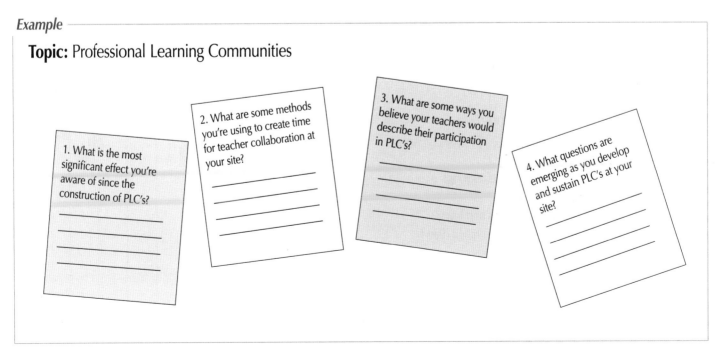

1. What is the most significant effect you're aware of since the construction of PLC's?

2. What are some methods you're using to create time for teacher collaboration at your site?

3. What are some ways you believe your teachers would describe their participation in PLC's?

4. What questions are emerging as you develop and sustain PLC's at your site?

Mapping Highs and Lows

Logistics

Materials and Preparation

Lay out a grid of five horizontal lines spanning the length of a full wall (masking tap or yarn works well for this purpose). Using the center line as the baseline, label the lines above +1 and +2 and the lines below –1 and –2. Divide the wall into time segments, again using masking tape or preprinted labels. Place sticky notes of two different colors on the tables. Each participant will need three notes of each color.

PowerPoint® direction slides

Time

30–45 minutes

Grouping: 4–6, full group

Tip

Model specific examples of highs and lows, including some differences in scaling (moderately high–very high). Model placement of sticky notes on graph, as well.

Variation

Use this process to assess group development. Direct the group members to determine highs and lows of their own progress as a group.

Purpose

Mapping Highs & Lows structures an opportunity for shared reflection and assessment of events during a specified period of time. The strategy is effective at the midpoint or end of a project, or to reflect upon the whole or a particular part of the school year. The vivid data display generated by the group creates a focal point for dialogue.

Intention

This strategy provides a visual summary of multiple perspectives that focuses a group's dialogue about its own programs and progress. It also offers the opportunity for a deeper look at assumptions and frames of reference regarding a specific event, project or time period.

Instructions to Group Leader

1. Create task groups of 4–6, providing each participant with three sticky notes of each color.
2. Individually, each group member thinks of three high points related to the event or time period, and records them, one high per sticky note, using one color note.
3. Repeat this step, thinking about and recording three low or challenging points, using the second color sticky note.
4. Introduce the wall graph and explain that it is a rating scale of highs and lows across a time period.
5. After 4–5 minutes (to complete the individual reflection), have participants post their sticky notes on the appropriate spot on the wall graph.
6. When all responses have been posted and the graph is complete, organize a group exploration of the data (see sample facilitator questions, below).

Example

Topic: Reflecting on the School Year

Sample Facilitator Questions:

How does this display compare to what you might have expected?

What are some patterns you're noticing?

What are some surprises?

How might you compare highs and lows?

What are some conclusions you might draw?

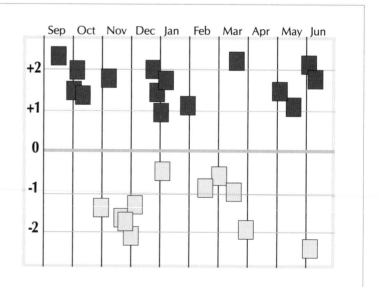

Paraphrase Passport

Purpose

Paraphrase Passport is a structured protocol for enhancing listening, increasing shared understanding and organizing dialogue. It is particularly effective for newly formed groups, or for any groups working with controversial or emotionally charged topics.

Intention

This strategy, originated by Spencer Kagan (1990) increases shared understanding and balanced participation by slowing the pace of a collaborative conversation and inserting a paraphrase. It builds community by ensuring that group members feel heard and understood.

Logistics

Materials and Preparation

A provocative question/ topic for groups to explore

PowerPoint® direction slides

Time

15–25 minutes

Grouping: Quartets

Instructions to Group Leader

1. Share the focus question/topic and give group members a minute or two to organize their thoughts. For example, "what are the most important factors influencing learning for all students?"

2. Model the protocol, emphasizing the insertion of a paraphrase before adding an idea and noting that the paraphrase can summarize several preceding comments – it does not have to only reflect the prior speaker.

3. Determine who will initiate the process by making a statement related to the question/topic. You can designate, or the group can choose.

4. Other group members must paraphrase the previous speaker(s) before adding related ideas, offering their opinion or perspective or asking a question.

5. Periodically, a group member might offer a summarizing and organizing paraphrase of the conversation as a whole.

Tips

Once you display the question/topic, ask group members to spend a minute or two organizing their thoughts in writing before beginning the dialogue.

Give groups an opportunity to check for understanding of the protocol before moving on with Step 2.

Variation

Insert a round-robin protocol (see page 89) so that participants speak and paraphrase in sequence, ensuring inclusion.

Three Step Interview

Logistics

Materials and Preparation

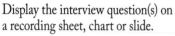

Determine an interview question, or several questions that will focus the conversation.

Display the interview question(s) on a recording sheet, chart or slide.

PowerPoint® direction slides

Time

15-20 minutes

Grouping: Pairs, quartets

Tips

It may be useful to provide the interview question(s) prior to the meeting, so participants have some time to think about their responses.

Remind partners that this is an interview to ensure that each speaker gets full attention for his or her thoughts and responses.

Variation

Use this protocol for participants to reflect on their growth as a group. For example, "What are some influences that the group work has had on my own practice?"

Purpose

Three Step Interview, developed by Spencer Kagan (1990), initially structures a paired exchange of knowledge, experience and perspectives on any given topic. The protocol then widens the frame by having pairs join other pairs for cross introductions and discussion.

Intention

This strategy balances participation and provides a time efficient method for examining information. It provides a foundation of shared information and an exchange of perspectives that, in many cases, illuminates thinking and clarifies understanding.

Instructions to Group Leader

1. Once partners are established, explain that this is an interview protocol, intended to provide time for each speaker to respond without interruption. Determine who will be the initial interviewer and who will respond.

2. Provide a relevant, engaging interview question, for example, "What are some of the most effective ways of increasing student engagement?"

3. Designate a time period for the first interview; and then signal when it is time for the pairs to switch roles.

4. Once each partner has been interviewed, form quartets (pairs squared). Group members introduce their partner and share a bit about their partner's responses.

What's The Problem? What's Not the Problem?

Purpose

What's The Problem? What's Not the Problem? is a dialogue and discussion tool for exploring messy issues. It is especially useful for engaging groups in addressing persistent and recurring issues or patterns that produce undesired outcomes. This structure guides group members in identifying root causes of the issue and separates out these elements from the more productive elements in the system. Adapted from *Silberman, 1999.*

Intention

This strategy widens perspectives by providing a psychologically safe environment for sharing and exploring the underlying factors that may be the sources of an issue or concern. It moves the group beyond the easy first explanations and breaks the patterns of blame or excuses that group members may be using to justify the current unproductive state of affairs.

Logistics

Materials and Preparation

Blank index cards

Chart or slide with question prompts for the dialogue

PowerPoint® direction slides

Time

30–40 minutes

Grouping: 4–6

Instructions to Group Leader

1. Identify a persistent problem or recurring issue.

2. Pose two prompts and have group members write brief responses on separate index cards.

    What's the problem?   What specifically is wrong?

    What is not the problem?

3. Have table group members first share their "What's not the problem?" cards and then develop a synthesizing statement and record it on a chart. Post the charts in view of the full group. Ask group members to share with their neighbors what they see as common elements in these charts. Invite volunteers to share their observations.

4. Next have table groups use their "What's the Problem?" cards as foundations for a deeper exploration of the issues. Use dialogue prompts below to structure this step.

5. For each statement offered push for the deeper related causal factors. Have table groups record these on charts.

6. Cluster the charts by prompt. Explore these charts to identify the deeper root causes.

7. Apply planning tools in previous sections to address these root causes. (See, for example, Outcome Mapping, page 29.)

Tips

Offer the dialogue prompts one at a time to encourage richer exploration of each question.

Variations

Have a different group member facilitate each dialogue prompt. Encourage the facilitator to paraphrase, summarize and organize the thinking of group members and then probe for clarification and elaboration of ideas.

Example

Dialogue Prompts:

Why does this problem occur and reoccur?
    Which is caused by…
    Which is caused by…
    Which is caused by…
Who is affected by this problem?
    Which then affects…
    Which then affects…
    Which then affects…

Who is not affected by this problem?
    Which then affects…
    Which then affects…
    Which then affects…
Where does this problem occur?
    It occurs there because…
Where does this problem not occur?
    It does not occur there because…

When does this problem occur?
    It occurs when…
When does this problem not occur?

Strategies for Generating Ideas

One strength of groups is the ability to generate lots of ideas. Ideas are the currency of group work or projects. Tasks, products and decisions improve when groups produce a wide menu of options from which to draw. Groups are more proficient at idea generation than individuals. Productive groups require strategies that balance engagement and open space for everyone's thinking, not just those who are most passionate, energized or opinionated.

There are predictable dynamics related to idea generation, including thinking in categories, vying between concrete and abstract ways of thinking, applying wide or narrow perspectives, and relying on the familiar rather than exploring the novel. Specific strategies that capture and stretch each and all of these dynamics are necessary for productive group work.

Well-designed strategies stimulate idea generation and reignite productivity when energy flags. These strategies also counter non-productive patterns, including dominance by individuals, digression via anecdote, and criticism of others' ideas.

To boost productivity and engagement, groups need structures for brainstorming, sorting, categorizing, qualifying, visualizing and envisioning. These mutually generated idea banks become shared resources for planning, problem solving and decision making processes.

The strategies that follow stimulate rich idea production and secure a space for all voices in the group to be included.

NOTE: Generating ideas is an important process and generally sequences with other functions. For example, the strategies described here can be stacked with an activator, an information processing strategy and, ultimately, a summarizer to create a full session design.

Brainstorm and Categorize

Logistics

Materials and Preparation

Chart paper, felt tip marker

PowerPoint® direction slides

Time

15–20 minutes

Grouping: 4–6

Purpose

Brainstorm and Categorize is an effective way to activate and share participants' prior knowledge and experience. Once ideas are generated, the group's thinking can be extended by organizing the information into categories that make sense to all members.

Intention

This strategy widens the knowledge base for individuals and groups. The idea generation process surfaces knowledge and the charts offer a visual display of the current thinking or working knowledge of each task group.

Tip

Identify a recorder for each group before the brainstorming begins.

Variations

Have each group record and post their ideas and categories on large charts. Items can be added as the topic continues to be explored or by other groups during a walk-about (see page 90).

Groups can use the categories they have generated to create a value statement about an initiative or a synthesizing statement related to a topic.

During the categorization phase, have group members explore the assumptions individuals are bringing to the ideas.

Have groups brainstorm and categorize questions, instead of ideas or items.

Instructions to Group Leader

1. Direct groups to brainstorm as many ideas as possible on a given topic. Note: You may opt for a Brainstorm and Pass pattern (see page 89) to balance participation.

2. After a designated amount of time, participants organize the individual items into categories.

3. Once categories are established, groups determine a label for each.

Example

Topic: Assessment Tools

Quizzes	Student surveys	
Homework	Student goal setting	
Class discussions	Rubrics	
Quick writes	SAT exam	
Exit slips	Categories	
End of chapter tests	Summative Assessments	
Benchmark tests	Formative Assessments	

Summative Assessments

Carousel Brainstorming

Purpose

Carousel Brainstorming engages the group in movement and collaborative learning. It infuses physical energy and is designed to link and extend knowledge and experience as small groups move from chart to chart generating information and building on previously constructed ideas.

Intention

This interactive and inclusive strategy taps the knowledge base of each participant and creates a shared base of information for further processing.

Instructions to Group Leader

1. Create task groups of 4–5. Give each group a different color marker that will travel with the group so their work can be identified on each chart.

2. Next, direct group members to a starting point at one of the charts. Be sure a starting recorder is identified in each group.

3. Each group brainstorms information related to the question/topic on the chart heading, recording as they work.

4. After an appropriate time interval, approximately 4–5 minutes, signal groups to rotate one station to the right.
   Note: The recording task can also rotate at this point.

5. Repeat the process at each station until groups are in front of their starting chart.

6. Groups review the information on their original chart and prepare any questions that might occur to them.

Logistics

Materials and Preparation

Post large sheets of newsprint, with a question or topic at the top, at various stations around the room (one chart for each task group).

Have masking tape, additional blank chart paper, and felt-tip markers available.

PowerPoint® direction slides

Time

25–30 minutes

Grouping: 4–5, full group

Tip

Suggest that groups use a Brainstorm and Pass pattern (see page 89) to ensure inclusion of all members.

Variations

Have the group generate the chart headings based on their questions, interests or concerns related to the topic.

When they return to their original chart, have groups categorize the information recorded there.

Create a random rotation by adding one more chart than the number of groups. A group can then move to any open chart when they are ready.

Example

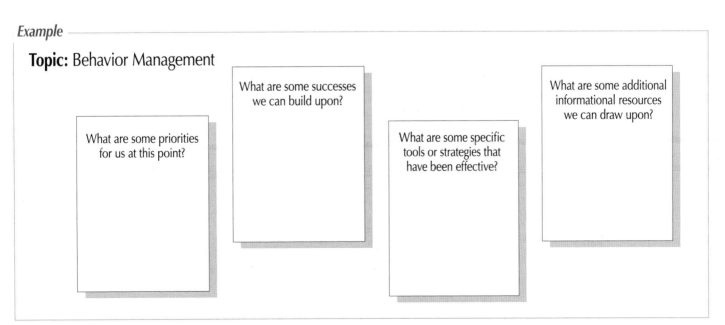

Topic: Behavior Management

What are some successes we can build upon?

What are some additional informational resources we can draw upon?

What are some priorities for us at this point?

What are some specific tools or strategies that have been effective?

Color Question Brainstorming

Logistics

Materials and Preparation

Use chart stands or post large sheets of newsprint at various stations around the room (one chart for each task group).

Have masking tape, additional blank chart paper, and felt-tip markers available.

PowerPoint® direction slides

Time

25–30 minutes

Grouping: 4–5, full group

Tips

Suggest that groups use a Brainstorm and Pass pattern (see page 89) to ensure inclusion of all members.

Abbreviate and synchronize the brainstorming period. For example, after groups have worked on one chart for 5 minutes or so, call time and direct them to another chart.

Variations

Insert a walk-about between Steps 3 and 4 so groups can learn from each other's thinking.

Purpose

Color Question Brainstorming supports both dialogue and discussion by generating questions rather than answers. The brainstorming pattern keeps it psychologically safe for participants to engage while the focus on exploring questions keeps thinking flexible and fluent.

Intention

This interactive and inclusive strategy both taps and stretches the different work style preferences of group members by requiring a specific mode of question generation at a given time. Brainstorming keeps it psychologically safe and keeps minds open to new possibilities. Colleagues gain insight into one another and grow to appreciate the different thinking styles available in the group.

Instructions to Group Leader

1. Create task groups of 4–5. Explain the question categories, as follows:

   Green Questions: Imagination, Ingenuity, Possibility

   Red Questions: Facts, Figures, Data

   Blue Questions: Judgments, Opinions, Values, Needs

2. Next, direct group members to brainstorm a large quantity of questions (without qualifying or judging them) beginning with whichever chart they choose, working with one chart/one category at a time, and moving on when ready.

3. After a designated amount of time (approximately 20 minutes), groups examine their lists, highlighting the questions that seem most relevant to the issue at hand.

4. Additional questions may be added at this time.

Example

Topic: Restructuring the School Schedule

Green	**What might happen if we...** What might happen if we changed the school schedule to create longer days in a four-day week?
Red	**How many... /How much...** How many hours of instruction time are possible with a four-day week? How many districts are using a four-day schedule?
Blue	**Why is this... /What's the best way to...** What is the optimal length of class periods per day in a four-day schedule? What are the best ways to manage teacher and student energy in a longer school day?

Idea, Category, Web

Purpose

Idea, Category, Web combines the classic strategies of brainstorming and visual organizers to extend and organize a group's thinking. The hands-on chart work provides a focus for group attention and energy.

Intention

This strategy amplifies the power of brainstorming by organizing the multiple ideas produced into categories for further exploration and application. It scaffolds complex cognitive tasks by breaking them into step-by-step stages and provides inclusion of all voices and readiness for continued work related to the topic being considered.

Logistics

Materials and Preparation

Prepare a T-chart, with one column labeled "Idea" and the other "Category."

Chart paper and markers

PowerPoint® direction slides

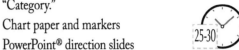

Time

25–30 minutes

Note: Allow an additional 10 minutes for modeling the first time this protocol is applied

Grouping: 4–6

Tip

It is very important to model the full process before task groups work independently. Use a non-threatening topic, such as television programs or a large city, for this purpose.

Instructions to Group Leader

1. Share the task directions with the group to provide a general idea of the multiple steps.

   Model the strategy as follows:

   IDEA/CATEGORY

   • Prepare a T-chart. Label the columns "Idea" and "Category."

   • Present a topic for idea and category generation. Call on a group member to offer an idea. Record it in the idea column.

   • Ask the same group member, or another participant to name the category within which the idea fits. Record the category name in the category column.

   • Once the category is recorded, check the idea column to be sure that there is at least one additional item that would fit this category.

   Note: Each category may be used only once. The goal is to generate broad categories for elaboration during the webbing phase.

   • Continue the process, developing six to eight categories.

   WEB

   • On a separate sheet of chart paper, create a web placing the main topic in the center with each category branching out from it.

   • Transfer the individual ideas for each category to the web; add additional ideas at this point.

2. Using a different topic, direct groups to apply the process on their own.

3. After a designated amount of time, create a walk-about (see page 90) or some other way for group members to view others' work and then review and refine their own.

Example

Topic: Reading in the Content Areas

IDEA	CATEGORY
think aloud	Text to Self
previewing for text features	Before Reading Strategies
summarizing statements	During Reading Strategies
naming main idea	After Reading Strategies

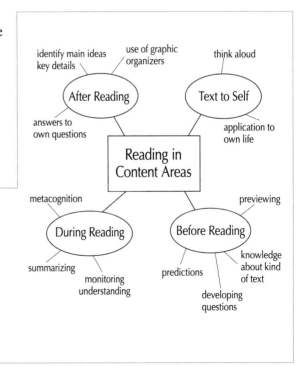

Round the Room and Back Again

Logistics

Materials and Preparation

Be ready with a topic or question.

Blank note paper

PowerPoint® direction slides

Time

15 minutes

Grouping: 3–6

Tips

Consider using this strategy instead of a formal break when both time and energy are limited.

This is an effective strategy to mark transitions between topics, as well as when introducing a new one.

Model some appropriate examples to get started. Examples should be short, succinct and easy to remember.

Variations

Use as an activator at a transition point to a new topic within a longer session.

Use this protocol for participants to reflect on their growth as a group (for example, "Ways the group added to my learning…,"or "Things that made this session productive…").

Purpose

Round the Room and Back Again engages group members' knowledge and experience as well as their energy. It sets up an exchange of information in preparation for further exploration, and can be applied to a wide range of topics, at the beginning, middle or end of a meeting or work session.

Intention

This interactive strategy provides physical energy and surfaces individual perspectives, knowledge and experience. It creates a shared base of information for further processing that emerges from the group members.

Instructions to Group Leader

1. Be sure each group member is ready with something to write on and something to write with. Let them know that they are going to begin a list, writing the first example and collecting additional information from colleagues in the room.

2. After writing one example of the topic for exploration have group members set their paper aside and move around the room, sharing their examples and collecting examples from others *without writing them down*. Note: The challenge is to rely on auditory memory. This motivates attentive listening and an efficient transition to the next step.

3. After two minutes or so, call time and direct participants to return to their seats and write down all of the examples they can recall.

4. At your signal, table groups pool their examples and create one extended list.

Example

Sample Lists:

Strategies to begin meetings

Ways data impacts instruction

Things I've applied since last meeting

Questions about implementing _____

Sort Cards

Purpose

Sort Cards can be used with a wide variety of topics to generate and then organize ideas, determining either part to whole, or whole to part relationships between concepts, terms or discrete items (e.g. data points, observations).

Intention

This strategy supports groups in generating and organizing information. The physical manipulation of the materials creates a high level of interaction and a concrete method for sharing perspectives and clarifying understanding.

Logistics

Materials and Preparation

Blank index cards or sticky notes
PowerPoint® direction slides

Time

20–30 minutes

Grouping: 4–6

Instructions to Group Leader

1. Direct individual group members to create a stack of cards, including associations, ideas or examples related to a specific topic. Note: Each item should be recorded on a separate card.

2. After approximately 5 minutes, begin a round-robin sharing (see page 89) of items, placing each card in the center of the table once its been shared.

3. Direct groups to sort their cards into stacks that make sense to all members of the group, based on the relationships they perceive between items.

4. Once the cards are sorted, groups create labels for each stack.

Tip

Be sure to ask task teams to articulate their reason for a particular grouping.

Variations

Have each group pass its stack of completed cards to another group for sorting.

Given a set of categories, have groups create their sort cards, using a Brainstorm and Pass structure (see page 89).

Once stacks are labeled, conduct a walk-about (see page 90) so groups can see each other's work.

Example

Topic: Formative Assessment

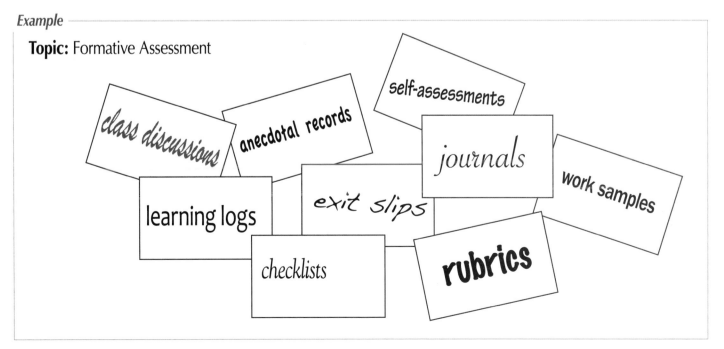

Strategies for Summarizing and Synthesizing

Head nods and smiles during a session don't always indicate understanding, agreement and readiness for action. Ending a meeting by providing participants with opportunities to clarify understanding, perceptions and next steps increases satisfaction and commitment to future action. Group members need an opportunity to express what they are taking away, how they will use new information and what they will do next. These personal and collective summaries increase transfer and application.

Strategies for summarizing and synthesizing support the integration of ideas and information. Summarizing produces a concise review of main points and sorting of critical information from nonessential details. Synthesizing integrates information into a cohesive whole, connecting disparate ideas and concepts and increasing the likelihood of effective application. Both cognitive processes are important to further task achievement and relational development for a group.

Summarizing and synthesizing strategies allow group members to describe to what degree they understand, agree and are ready to move forward. Giving individual perspectives a public voice offers a values-check within and across group members and develops a deeper understanding of oneself and others. These statements also provide information to the group leader about the group's current state.

There is often a high distraction factor at the end of a meeting. People mentally and emotionally start to leave the room. Over-packed agendas and poorly implemented processes during the meeting squeeze out summarizing and synthesizing opportunities. These important elements get eliminated when groups run out of time, energy, and interest.

Planning the flow of meetings or work sessions to protect time for summary and synthesis is critical. The strategies that follow scaffold these essential thinking processes. This culminating connection-making creates a bridge between what happens in the meeting and what happens in practice.

NOTE: Many of the summarizing and synthesizing strategies described in this section can also be used as activators.

3-2-1

Logistics

Materials and Preparation

Duplicate 3-2-1 worksheet for each group member.

PowerPoint® direction slides

Time

15–20 minutes

Grouping: 4–6

Purpose

3-2-1 can be used with a wide variety of topics to summarize understanding and increase retention and transfer of new information at a meeting's close. The structured worksheet, individual think time and shared exchange increase focus and engagement. This strategy is also effective at the start of a session to activate readiness.

Intention

This strategy promotes the individual integration of ideas while developing and expanding the shared knowledge base. Individual preparation time increases balance and inclusion in the sharing stage.

Tips

To preserve meeting time, the 3-2-1 worksheets can be completed prior to the session.

Have groups begin sharing with one category. After each table group member has shared something in that category, then move on to the others.

Ask table groups to choose a member to share for their table as they prepare their report.

Variations

Use 3-2-1 for goal setting by making the '1' item be a goal statement.

Add a column (+1) for structuring and recording shared ideas.

Instructions to Group Leader

1. Direct individuals to complete their 3-2-1 recording sheets.

2. After 5–8 minutes, table groups then share and explore their ideas, using a round-robin process (see page 89) to ensure balanced participation.

3. After approximately 10 minutes, ask each group to choose some aspect of their conversation to share with the full group. Give them two minutes to organize their report.

Example

3-2-1

3 · Facts

2 · Questions

1 · Main Idea

3 · Facts   +1

2 · Questions

1 · Main Idea

Elevator Speech

Purpose

An **Elevator Speech** is a way of closing a meeting by having group members construct and then share with a partner their personal summaries of the processes, outcomes and next steps the group developed during the session.

Intention

This strategy provides individuals with the opportunity to develop and share their own summaries of a meeting or session. Elevator speeches are intended to be short and succinct since you only have a brief time to get your point across. By sharing this speech with others, memories of what occurred become strengthened and participants gain insight into what others in the room are noticing and reflecting upon.

Logistics

Materials and Preparation

Index Cards

Public Timer

PowerPoint® direction slides

Time

10–15 minutes depending on full group size

Grouping: Pairs

Instructions to Group Leader

1. At the closing segment of a session, pause and ask participants to silently reflect on essential aspects of the session's processes, outcomes and agreed on next steps.
2. Introduce the concept of an elevator speech, distribute index cards and have participants craft their own relevant examples.
3. After the allotted writing time, form pairs and have participants rehearse their elevator speeches.
4. If time allows, ask volunteers to share their speeches with the larger group.

Tips

Use a public timer to help keep groups on task.

Be sure to protect enough time for this process, especially if emotions are running high and/or the group has made a significant breakthrough in its work. Protecting time for sharing is especially important when using the variation noted below.

Variation

Use this strategy to help participants prepare and rehearse what they will communicate to others outside the meeting room when important decisions or action steps need to be shared with a wider audience. For this use, be sure to have volunteers share their contributions with the larger group after they have rehearsed with a partner. Or have individuals nominate their partners to share with the larger group.

Generate, Sort, Synthesize

Logistics

Materials and Preparation

Blank index cards

PowerPoint® direction slides

Time

20–30 minutes

Grouping: 4–6

Purpose

Generate, Sort, Synthesize can be used with a wide variety of topics to explore relationships between discrete pieces of information. Then the tool can be used to organize the information into larger categorical or conceptual groupings.

Intention

This multistep strategy structures exploration and synthesis of information, while incorporating and honoring individual points of view. The physical manipulation of the materials creates a high level of interaction and a concrete method for sharing perspectives and clarifying understanding.

Tips

Give directions one step at a time so groups don't move too quickly into creating categories, which might reduce the depth of exploration of ideas during Step 2.

Give several examples of synthesizing statements or provide a template for their construction.

Variations

Have each group work on a different topic or subtopic.

Once clusters are labeled, conduct a walk-about (see page 90) so groups can see each other's thinking before creating their synthesis.

Instructions to Group Leader

1. Direct individuals to generate 3–5 ideas related to the topic, placing each idea on a separate index card.

2. Table groups share and explore these ideas using a round-robin process (see page 89) to ensure balanced participation.

3. Groups sort their cards into clusters that make sense to all members of the group, based on the relationships they perceive between items.

4. Once the cards are sorted, the group creates labels for each cluster.

5. Finally, ask each group to create a synthesizing statement, incorporating the ideas explored during the previous steps, and reflecting big ideas, discoveries and insights related to the topic.

Example

Topic: Effective Meetings

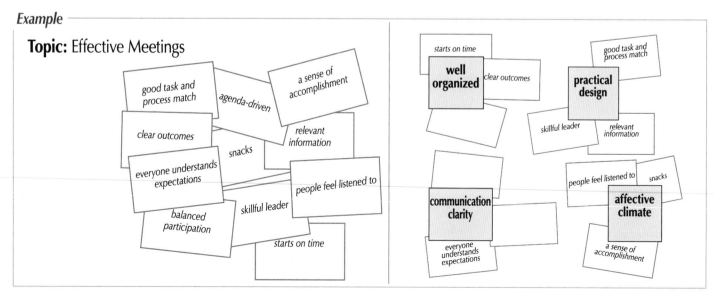

Invent an App

Purpose

Invent an App taps into participants' familiarity with current communications tools by offering a creative way to summarize essential understandings at key junctures in meetings or learning sessions. Smartphone apps provide accessible tools and quick connections to important people and information resources. This strategy is also effective for activating prior knowledge at the start of a session.

Intention

This strategy focuses energy and attention by providing an engaging scaffold for organizing and synthesizing information using the contemporary metaphor of an app.

Instructions to Group Leader

1. Introduce the concept of an app by naming their essential functions: providing tools, access to resource people and access to information. To design an app means that participants should think of an essential resource that they would like to have in their pocket or purse to pull out at critical moments in their working day. Apps require a catchy name, an icon, a purpose and a variety of functions.

2. Name a time frame for completion of first drafts.

3. Invite participants to share their apps with the larger group.

Logistics

Materials and Preparation

Blank note paper

Chart paper

Public timer

PowerPoint® direction slides

Time

10–15 minutes depending on full group size

Grouping: 3–6

Tips

Use a public timer to help keep group members on task.

Have groups pull out smartphones and use their features to stimulate idea production.

Variation

If time permits, especially at the end of a longer session or series, have groups illustrate their apps on chart paper showing the name, icon and key functions.

Example

Topic: App for a Decision Making Meeting

Name: Conflict Buster
Icon: Two rams butting heads
Functions:
1. Biofeedback settings to help the holder control pulse and respiration.
2. Speed dial connection to a coaching voice fed into a hidden earpiece.
3. Emotion filter that removes the negative or confrontational tone from the voices of speakers.
4. Reframer tool that listens for the positive intentions in negative comments.

Introducing... **CONFLICT BUSTER**

With
Biofeedback Settings
Speed Dial
Emotion Filter
Reframer Tool

Key Words

Logistics

Materials and Preparation
PowerPoint® direction slides

Time
5–10 minutes

Grouping: 4–6

Purpose

Key Words is a time-efficient strategy for organizing the learning for individuals and the group. It provides an opportunity for each group member to contribute a synthesizing word to be shared and explored with a table group.

Intention

This strategy gives individual group members a chance to reflect on what was important to them, and to hear what was important to others. It also provides feedback to the leader about what the individual group members are remembering and valuing.

Tip

Foreshadow this strategy at an earlier point in the session to increase group members' consciousness about the content and processes they are experiencing.

Instructions to Group Leader

1. Ask group members to reflect on the session and select a key word that for them captures an important idea or concept. The word might reflect content or emotion.

2. Using a round-robin pattern (see page 89), have group members share their key word and why they selected it.

3. After a designated time invite each table group to nominate one member to share his or her key word with the larger group.

Variation

Have each table group produce a chart listing their key words.

Most Important Point

Purpose

Most Important Point is a time-efficient strategy for reinforcing the learning for individuals and the group. It provides an opportunity for each group member to surface and express significant ideas related to the topic and to hear the ideas generated by others.

Intention

This strategy gives individual group members a chance to surface essential content and hear what was significant to others. It also provides feedback to the leader about what the group retains and/or values.

Logistics

Materials and Preparation
PowerPoint® direction slides

Time
5–10 minutes

Grouping: 2–6

Instructions to Group Leader

1. Ask individuals to produce a key point or significant idea they've derived from the session thus far; what they consider to be the Most Important Point (M.I.P.).

2. After 1–2 minutes, have group members share their M.I.P., with a partner or with their table group.

Variations

Direct participants to paraphrase their colleague's M.I.P. before sharing their own, whether in partners or table groups.

After pairs share their M.I.P.'s, use a Partner's Report pattern (see page 89) to share with the full group or ask table groups to choose one M.I.P. to share with the full group.

Use the same protocol to generate a Most Important Criteria as a dialogue tool prior to a decision-making discussion.

One Word Summary

Logistics

Materials and Preparation
PowerPoint® direction slides

Time:
5–10 minutes

Grouping: 4–6

Purpose

One Word Summary is a time-efficient strategy for organizing the learning for individuals and the group. It provides an opportunity for each group member to contribute a synthesizing word to be discussed with a task group.

Intention

This strategy gives individual group members a chance to reflect on what was important to them, and to hear what was important to others. It also provides feedback to the leader about what the group retains and/or values.

Tip

Ask groups to identify a reporter, who will share their word. This level of readiness helps to maintain momentum when sharing out, especially with a large group.

Variation

You might give individuals time to create their own one-word summary before the task group's discussion.

Instructions to Group Leader

1. Ask task groups to develop a one-word summary of the session which might reflect content or emotion.

2. Give groups 3–4 minutes to decide on one that they will share with the full group.

3. After the designated time, orchestrate a full-group share.

Scrambled Sentences

Purpose

Scrambled Sentences close a meeting or learning experience by capturing and sharing important idea from the session. This high energy strategy provides opportunities for individual and collective synthesis with a ceremonial spirit for ending a session.

Intention

This strategy focuses energy and attention by providing a clear structure for integrating ideas and information from a session. Scrambled Sentences provides each participant with a means for contributing to the final summary of the session and builds community through group member interaction and sharing.

Logistics

Materials and Preparation

An index card for each participant
PowerPoint® direction slides

Time

10–15 minutes depending on full group size

Grouping: Quartets, full group

Instructions to Group Leader

1. Distribute index cards and instruct each participant to record a keyword that captures an important idea from the session.
2. Have participants leave their tables and move around the room greeting others.
3. Signal a halt and instruct participants to form groups of four and share their key words. Have the groups eliminate any duplicates and substitute other appropriate key words.
4. Direct the groups of four to craft a sentence using their keywords.
5. Form a circle around the perimeter of the room and have each group share their sentences with verbal and nonverbal emphasis to indicate each key word as it emerges in the sentence.

Tips

Line up the quartet members to match the order of the keywords in their sentences. This adds to the clarity of the presentations.

Suggest that groups practice their sentence and add verbal and nonverbal impact to their presentation.

Variation

If time permits, especially at the end of longer sessions or series, have quartets write their Scrambled Sentences on chart paper with the key words emphasized. Post these on the wall.

Snowball Fight

Logistics

Materials and Preparation

Blank slips of paper for creating snowballs

PowerPoint® direction slides

Time

10–15 minutes depending on full group size

Grouping: Full group

Purpose

Snowball Fight is a high energy strategy that engages all participants in summarizing their experiences, and provides a ceremonial end to a meeting or learning session. Individual group members create "snowballs" of crumpled paper after writing synthesizing statements on them in preparation for a full-group exchange.

Intention

This strategy balances individual integration of ideas with an appreciation of the ideas of others. The playful nature of the snowball fight infuses energy and builds community.

Tip

Three snowballs is the maximum. You can move on to step three as long as everyone has at least one idea crafted.

Variations

Adjust the template to fit the context of your meeting.

Adjust the number of snowballs to fit your time frame.

Instructions to Group Leader

1. Display a slide or chart with a template for crafting snowballs, as follows:

    A thank you (expressing appreciation for something the group contributed to your experience)

    A principle of practice ("always remember to…,"or "its important to…")

    A wish (for group members)

2. Provide 3–4 minutes for individuals to record their thoughts on three slips of paper, one idea per slip.

3. Create snowballs by crumpling each slip of paper.

4. Explain that at the start signal participants will throw their snowballs and scoop up new ones as they land, continuing to throw them until the stop signal.

5. At the stop signal each group member picks up three snowballs and returns to a table group where members share what they've retrieved.

6. Each group chooses one thought to share aloud with the full group to end the meeting.

Example

Topic: A Workshop on Literacy Strategies

Thank you for sharing your effective applications.
Always remember to assess where students are and plan accordingly.
I wish you enough challenges to learn from as you apply new strategies with your students; but not enough to cause frustration.

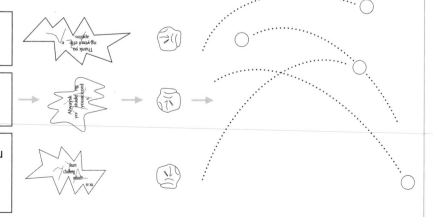

Swap Meet

Purpose

Swap Meet ends a meeting or work session with an exchange of specific examples or applications related to the topic. Swap Meet can also be used to begin a work session in preparation for further exploration.

Intention

This interactive strategy provides physical energy and increases the likelihood of transfer to practice. It creates a shared base of information for further processing that emerges from the group members.

Logistics

Materials and Preparation

Be ready with a topic, sentence stem or question.

Index or blank note cards

PowerPoint® direction slides

Time

15 minutes

Grouping: 4–6

Instructions to Group Leader

1. Direct individuals to fill in a card with an answer to a question, or a completion of a sentence stem that requires an example or application. For example, "one thing I intend to try..." or "one thing I want to be sure to remember...".

2. Once the cards are complete, direct group members to circulate around the room, sharing the information on their cards and then *exchanging* cards with their colleague. Note: Individuals leave with someone else's card.

3. After two or three exchanges, direct group members to return to their table and share the information on the card they have in hand.

4. Table groups identify themes and patterns to share with the full group.

Tips

Add an explicit direction to paraphrase the information being exchanged to ensure application of this important skill.

To save meeting time, group members can bring their ideas to swap to the meeting.

Variations

When a group is meeting for the first time, add identity information to the card (e.g., name, role, work site).

Use this protocol for participants to reflect on their growth as a group. (For example, "One way the group added to my learning...," or "What is one contribution you made to the group's productivity during this session?").

Tweets

Logistics

Materials and Preparation

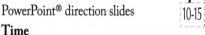

Blank note paper

Chart paper

Public timer

PowerPoint® direction slides

Time

10–15 minutes depending on full group size

Grouping: Pairs

Purpose

Tweets are a way of closing a meeting by having pairs of participants craft and then share with the larger group their personal summaries of the meeting and/or learning experiences. The strategy is based on the 140-character limitation used on Twitter.

Intention

This strategy focuses energy and attention by providing a clear structure for integrating ideas and information from a session. The character limit forces a succinct summary.

Tips

Use a public timer to help keep group members on task.

Remind participants that they can use conventional abbreviations and text-messaging conventions such as B4 (before) or L8R (later).

Variations

If time permits, especially at the end of longer sessions or series, have pairs write their Tweets on chart paper for posting on the wall.

Instructions to Group Leader

1. Introduce the concept of a Tweet by naming the character limitations imposed by Twitter: a maximum of a 140 characters, including all spaces and punctuation.

2. Name a timeframe for completion of first drafts.

3. Invite participants to share their Tweets with the larger group.

Example

Tweets tap into contemporary techno/cultural practices and help group members synthesize information using one hundred and forty characters.

Walk-About Survey

Purpose

Walk-About Survey involves the full group in an exchange of information. It infuses physical energy and is designed to link and extend knowledge and experience; moving from individual to full group to smaller group and back to individual again.

Intention

During this interactive strategy individuals surface and exchange perspectives, knowledge and new understandings based on their experience during a meeting or work session. Different thinking processes are intentionally applied at each step.

Logistics

Materials and Preparation

Create a survey grid and duplicate for each group member.

Public Timer

PowerPoint® direction slides

Time

25–30 minutes

Grouping: 4–6, full group

Instructions to Group Leader

1. Given the Walk-About Survey worksheet, individuals generate their own response for each category in the left-hand column of the page.

2. Direct group members to circulate and complete their page by surveying colleagues who are not in their own small group and capturing their thinking in each box. Note: Only one response should be collected from each person.

3. After a designated length of time, usually 10–12 minutes, participants return to their small groups and share the collected information as well as their own responses.

4. Once the information has been shared, small groups explore and analyze the collective responses for themes, comparisons, contrasts and generalizations.

5. Small groups look for patterns and themes and draw conclusions based on their exploration. Each small group prepares to share an observation and some conclusions or theories as to the reason for the identified result.

Tips

When time is limited during a meeting, have group members collect fewer responses, for example in a tic-tac-toe pattern.

Increase task focus by using a public timer at various stages.

Variations

Use this protocol for participants to reflect on their growth as a group. (For example, "my contribution to the group's growth," "my colleagues contribution to the group's growth," or "a goal area for us as a group.")

Example

TOPIC: _____

Effective category possibilities include:

Positive results, negative results, interesting results

Key points, significant ideas, questions

Concerns, hopes, stumbling blocks

NAME	NAME	NAME
NAME	NAME	NAME
NAME	NAME	NAME

Strategies for Text and Information Processing

Using resources and reaching out to the research base informs dialogue, discussion, planning and problem-solving. Structuring the interaction between group members and text creates a psychologically safe environment for sharing and exploring individual perspectives, experiences, connections and questions.

Implementing thoughtfully designed protocols with relevant information sources promotes the social construction of knowledge so group members can learn with and from the text and with and from one another. Providing equal access to information develops a shared knowledge base and gives individuals the confidence to counter opinions not encumbered by facts, and eliminates the confusion between personal relationships and ideas. Building on this foundation enhances the ultimate outcomes and satisfaction with the group work.

Drawing on external points of reference increases capacity for grappling with complex issues. The interactions with text and colleagues produce a wider frame of reference to individual concerns. When groups are limited by their own experiences and perspectives, the meeting becomes a serial pat on the back that reinforces present practices and beliefs. Using text, and other materials, as a source of expertise counters this tendency toward self-confirming logic.

Some group leaders are reluctant to use text-based protocols because the cost of preparation time and selecting the appropriate text and strategy can seem prohibitive. Expending time in the session for silent reading can seem cumbersome as well. The alternative of asking group members to read ahead also seems risky. However, when group members engage in structured interaction with text, they discover the value of these strategies. The compelling benefits include engagement, readiness, balance, productivity and more satisfying use of meeting time.

The use of text without structure (i.e., read an article and talk) opens the door for disengagement and for dominant voices to prevail. The strategies that follow encourage balanced participation, structure time efficiently and promote high engagement with text; elements that are critical for success.

NOTE: Processing information is an important function and generally sequences with other functions. The strategies described here are enhanced by stacking them between an activator and a summarizer.

A-B Each Teach

Logistics

Materials and Preparation

Choose and duplicate for each participant a piece of text that has two or more key chunks of information.

Public timer

PowerPoint® direction slides

Time

15–20 minutes depending on the reading

Grouping: Pairs

Purpose

A-B Each Teach is a paired reading strategy that has a jigsaw quality in that each partner reads and teaches the other. Through this exchange partners develop clear understandings and concrete examples or applications from text-based material.

Intention

This strategy increases personal accountability and focuses attention on critical details while examining information. Paired work and a brief time frame make this strategy useful for exploring cognitively complex topics. It builds a foundation of shared information, illuminates thinking and clarifies understanding.

Tips

Choose a reading selection that is not too long, relevant to your group's work and lends itself to segmentation.

Be sure partners sit side-by-side so the text is a focusing point for their conversation, and to minimize room volume.

Focus and support success by providing a structured sheet for preparing to teach.

Variations

Once the Each Teach is complete, assign a task for partners to complete together to demonstrate their understanding of the entire text selection.

Use this protocol with other focusing materials, such as data, student work products, rubrics, lesson plans.

Instructions to Group Leader

1. Have partners letter off A and B.

2. Explain that each partner will read a segment of a larger selection and prepare to teach the information.

3. Provide 10 minutes for reading and preparing to teach. Each partner should include: a summary statement, key points, and concrete examples or applications in their lesson.

4. After the designated time, begin the Each Teach session.

Example

- Summary

- Key Points

- Examples/Applications

Focused Reading

Purpose

Focused Reading purposefully engages readers with the text, causing them to compare and contrast their personal knowledge base with the new information.

Intention

This strategy increases attention to text-based information, and supports contextualization of the information to the reader's own work. It also provides a scaffold for participant interaction related to the text.

Logistics

Materials and Preparation

Choose and duplicate for each participant an appropriate piece of text.

PowerPoint® direction slides

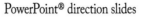

Time

15–25 minutes including discussion, depending on the reading

Grouping: Pairs or quartets

Instructions to Group Leader

1. Introduce the participants to the focused reading annotations

   √ = Got it. I know or understand this

   ! = This is really important information

   ? = I'd like clarification or elaboration of this material

2. Assign a text passage for reading and marking.

3. After reading, organize pairs or quartets to share and compare their responses.

Tip

Ask participants to read and annotate the text selection outside of the meeting setting. This allows for individual pacing and preserves meeting time for more face-to-face exchange.

Variations

Structure the exchange of information (Step 3 above) using a 3-2-1 (see page 64) or Walk-About Survey protocol (see page 75).

Use this protocol with other focusing materials, such as data sets, student work samples, or curriculum documents. Create different annotation symbols as needed.

Example

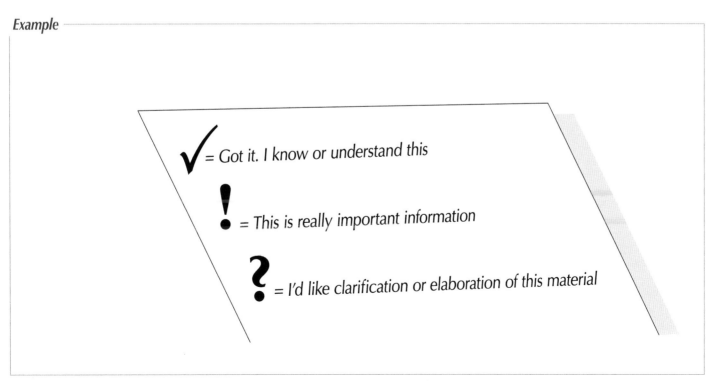

√ = Got it. I know or understand this

! = This is really important information

? = I'd like clarification or elaboration of this material

Key Concepts, Key Ideas

Logistics

Materials and Preparation

Choose and duplicate for each participant an appropriate piece of text.

Public timer

PowerPoint® direction slides

Time

15–20 minutes depending on the reading

Grouping: Pairs

Purpose

Key Concepts, Key Ideas is a paired reading strategy for constructing meaning from text-based information. In this strategy, individuals explore the entire selection and reflect on their own before sharing and exploring ideas with a partner. The part to whole approach of this strategy is effective with text structures that are not easily segmented. It also makes a good fit with some work style preferences.

Intention

This strategy gives each partner a sense of the whole before analyzing selected ideas with a partner. Idea exploration, supported by attentive listening and active inquiry enhances individual and shared understanding.

Tips

Choose a reading selection that is not too long and relevant to your group's work with enough complexity to support deep examination.

For experienced groups and/or groups that are familiar with this strategy, the reading and highlighting task can be completed as preparation for the session to maximize work session time.

Be sure partners sit side-by-side so the text is a focusing point for their conversation and to minimize room volume.

Variation

Use this protocol with other focusing materials such as data, student work products, teaching/learning standards, curriculum documents.

Instructions to Group Leader

1. Explain to group members that they will be reading a text selection individually and highlighting words or short phrases that capture important or interesting ideas.

2. Once each partner has read through and marked the text, pairs share and discuss highlighted items, taking turns initiating the ideas for exploration.

3. As part of their exploration, ask pairs to identify new thinking and any questions that have emerged.

4. After the designated amount of time, widen the conversation (configure quartets, table groups or full group).

Prompt and Respond

Purpose

Prompt and Respond is a paired reading strategy for engaging with text-based information. This strategy incorporates incremental stopping points for responding to question prompts that cause readers to process the information in various ways, (e.g., summarize, apply, connect to their own practice). Through structured exchanges, partners share their responses. This thinking out loud and co-generation of ideas enhances individual and shared understanding.

Intention

This strategy uses individual and collaboratively written responses to process information and ideas presented in text. The deliberate process of reading, thinking, talking and writing increases depth of understanding and clarifies and personalizes concepts.

Instructions to Group Leader

1. Explain to partners that they will be reading individually until they reach a prompt, at which point they consider and discuss their response with their partner.
2. After partnered exploration, individuals take a minute or so to record thoughts.
3. Partners continue this process until the selection is completed.
4. After the designated amount of time, widen the conversation (configure quartets, table groups or full group).

Logistics

Materials and Preparation

Choose an appropriate piece of text and intersperse specific prompts at various stopping points.

Create a worksheet for recording responses or reproduce the text with embedded space for recording.

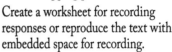

Public timer

PowerPoint® direction slides

Time

20–30 minutes depending on the reading

Grouping: Pairs

Tips

Choose a reading selection that is not too long, relevant to your group's work and lends itself to segmentation.

Be sure partners sit side-by-side so the text is a focusing point for their conversation and to minimize room volume.

Use this strategy as a scaffold to build confidence and readiness when launching a new initiative or change effort.

Variations

Individuals read the entire selection, recording their responses as they read. After a designated amount of time, partners exchange their thinking regarding each prompt or select specific prompts they would like to discuss.

Give individuals the reading and prompts ahead of the meeting and ask them to bring their recorded notes with them.

Read and Connect

Logistics

Materials

Choose and duplicate for each participant an appropriate piece of text and identify several stopping points.

Blank paper for recording connections

Public timer

PowerPoint® direction slides

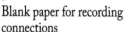

Time

20–30 minutes depending on the reading

Grouping: Trios

Tips

Choose material that is intended to be applicable to a practice.

Construct trios purposefully. For example, like-role or diverse roles, depending on your outcomes.

Use this strategy as a scaffold to build confidence and readiness when launching a new initiative or change effort.

Purpose

In **Read and Connect**, trios generate connections and applications while reading a text selection. This strategy incorporates incremental stopping points for these linkages. At each intersection, a group member summarizes and trios construct connections and applications to their work which enhances shared understanding and develops common reference points.

Intention

This strategy structures inclusion and balance of all voices in the group. Each member is accountable for organizing a specific aspect of the information and all are accountable for considering its use. This strategy supports and increases the likelihood of the transfer of ideas to individual practice.

Instructions to Group Leader

1. Ask trios to letter off A to C.

2. Explain that they will be reading individually to a designated stopping point and taking turns summarizing what's been read. At each pause and summary point, trios develop and record connections and applications to their own work.

3. Trios continue this process, alternating the summarizing and recording roles, until the selection is completed.

4. After the designated amount of time, widen the conversation (sextets or full group).

Read and Example

Purpose

Read and Example is a paired reading strategy for generating specific examples/applications from text-based information. This strategy incorporates incremental stopping points for generating examples. Through structured exchanges, partners develop these examples to clarify understanding of the text material. This thinking out loud and co-generation of ideas enhances individual and shared understanding.

Intention

This strategy balances participation and provides a time efficient method for developing concrete images of ideas presented in text. Paired work and a brief time frame makes this strategy effective for considering applications to practice. This strategy expands a foundation of shared information, clarifies and personalizes theory and increases likelihood of retention and transfer of new ideas.

Logistics

Materials and Preparation

Choose an appropriate piece of text and identify several stopping points.

Create a worksheet for recording examples with labels for each text segment.

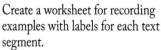

Public timer

PowerPoint® direction slides

Time

20–30 minutes depending on the reading

Grouping: Pairs

Instructions to Group Leader

1. Ask partners to letter off A and B.
2. Explain that they will be reading individually to a designated stopping point and taking turns summarizing what's been read. At each stop and summary point, partners co-develop examples that illustrate their understanding of the text.
3. Partners continue this process until the selection is completed.
4. After the designated amount of time, widen the conversation (configure quartets, table groups or full group).

Tips

Choose a reading selection that is not too long, relevant to your group's work and lends itself to segmentation.

Be sure partners sit side-by-side so the text is a focusing point for their conversation and to minimize room volume.

Use this strategy as a scaffold to build confidence and readiness when launching a new initiative or change effort.

Use a public timer to balance time, talk, and task completion.

Read-Share-Inquire

Logistics

Materials and Preparation

Choose an appropriate piece of text and identify several stopping points.

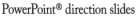

PowerPoint® direction slides

Time

20–30 minutes depending on the reading

Grouping: Pairs

Purpose

Read-Share-Inquire is a paired reading strategy for exploring values and beliefs, while exercising and developing group members' paraphrasing skills. This strategy incorporates incremental stopping points, helping to maintain balance and increase focus on the thinking of each partner in turn.

Intention

This strategy provides a low-risk structure for partners to examine the values that underlie their practice, personalizing content information for closer consideration. Paired work and the use of paraphrase makes this strategy effective for exploring cognitively complex and/or emotionally charged topics in a psychologically safe manner.

Tips

Choose a reading selection that is not too long, relevant to your group's work and lends itself to introspection regarding values.

To save time, ask group members to read the selection prior to attending the meeting.

Be sure partners sit side-by-side so the text is a focusing point for their conversation and to minimize room volume.

Use this strategy as a scaffold to build confidence and readiness when launching a new initiative or change effort.

Variation

Invite partners to choose a reading selection they want to explore. These can be from a reading list and do not have to be the same as other partners.

Instructions to Group Leader

1. Ask partners to letter off A and B.
2. Explain that they will be reading individually to a designated stopping point and then following a structured interview protocol, taking turns inquiring into the other's thinking, as follows:
   - Partner A shares a key point or connection.
   - Partner B paraphrases partner A and inquires:
     "And what makes that important to you?"
   - Partner B responds and then shares a key point or connection.
   - Partner A paraphrases partner B and inquires:
     "And what makes that important to you?"
3. Partners continue this process until the selection is completed.

Say Something

Purpose

Say Something is a paired reading strategy developed by Agawa and Harste (2001) for constructing meaning from text-based information. This strategy incorporates incremental stopping points to check for understanding. Through structured exchanges, partners develop relationships between new information and what they already know or believe. This thinking out loud, supported by attentive listening, enhances individual and shared understandings.

Intention

This strategy focuses attention, even when energy is low or distraction is high. It provides a time efficient and balanced method for examining information. This strategy provides a foundation of shared information and an exchange of perspectives that, in many cases, illuminates thinking and clarifies understanding.

Logistics

Materials and Preparation

Choose and duplicate for each participant an appropriate piece of text and identify several stopping points.

Public timer

PowerPoint® direction slides

Time

Varies depending on the reading; generally 15-20 minutes

Grouping: Pairs

Instructions to Group Leader

1. Explain to group members that they will be reading individually to a designated stopping point and then engaging in a brief exchange of ideas. These might include a brief summary, a key point, an interesting idea, a new connection or a question.

2. Once each partner has reached the chosen stopping point, partners pause and "Say Something" to each other. Note: The statement should be fairly brief and succinct.

3. Partners continue this process until the selection is completed.

4. After the designated amount of time, widen the conversation (configure quartets, table groups or full group).

Tips

Choose a reading selection that is not too long, relevant to your group's work and lends itself to segmentation.

Be sure partners sit side-by-side so the text is a focusing point for their conversation and to minimize room volume.

Use a public timer to balance time, talk and task completion.

Variations

Have partners decide together how far they will read before stopping and exchanging comments.

Use this protocol with other focusing materials such as data, student work products, rubrics, lesson plans.

Three A's Plus One

Logistics

Materials and Preparation

Choose an appropriate piece of text.

Four index cards for each participant

PowerPoint® direction slides

Time

30–40 minutes depending on the reading

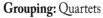

Grouping: Quartets

Purpose

Three A's Plus One is a small group reading strategy for exploring values, beliefs and assumptions, while exercising and developing group member's paraphrasing and inquiry skills. Each participant selects and records responses to specific prompts on separate index cards. This strategy includes a small group process in which each member of the quartet facilitates one round of inquiry.

Adapted from National School Reform Faculty.

Intention

This strategy structures a low-risk interaction during which quartets examine the beliefs and values that underlie their practice, personalizing content information for closer consideration. Small group work and the use of paraphrase and inquiry make this strategy effective for exploring cognitively complex and/or emotionally charged topics in a psychologically safe manner. The protocol develops and exercises facilitation skills as well.

Tips

Choose a reading selection that is not too long, relevant to your group's work and lends itself to introspection regarding values.

To save time, ask group members to read the selection prior to attending the meeting and fill out the first three cards.

Use this strategy as a scaffold to build confidence and readiness when launching a new initiative or change effort.

Variations

Invite quartets to choose a reading selection they want to explore. These can be from a reading list, and do not have to be the same as other quartets.

Instructions to Group Leader

1. Distribute the text selection and four index cards to each participant.
2. Participants then read the selection and on separate cards record:
   - One thing with which you **agree**
   - One thing with which you might **argue**
   - One thing to which you **aspire**

   Note: The fourth card's topic will be assigned later.
3. Ask quartet members to letter off A to D.
4. Round 1: Quartet members share their agreement cards without elaborating about why they choose that item and place their card on the table. When all four cards are on display, Person A offers a summarizing paraphrase of what has appeared there. He or she then leads an inquiry among the small group members about the values and beliefs they might be holding that influenced the choice of agreements.
5. Round 2: Quartet members repeat the process of sharing and inquiry by placing their argument cards on the table. Person B leads this round.
6. Round 3: Quartet members repeat the process of sharing and inquiry by placing their aspiration cards on the table. Person C leads this round.
7. Round 4: Quartet members take out their fourth index card and record personal "Aha's" such as insights or new perceptions that are emerging from their exploration of the content. Quartet members repeat the process of sharing and inquiry by placing their Aha cards on the table. Person D leads this round.
8. Invite quartet members to share some of their insights with the larger group.

Example

Sample Prompts

What are some of the connections between our agreements (aspirations, arguments, aha's)?

What might be some assumptions related to these agreements (aspirations, arguments, aha's)?

What might be some of our beliefs related to these agreements (aspirations, arguments, aha's)?

What be some implications for our work related to these agreements (aspirations, arguments, aha's)?

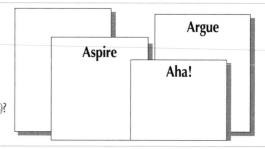

Words, Phrases, Sentences

Purpose

Words, Phrases, Sentences can be used with a wide variety of texts to explore relationships between discrete pieces of information and the greater meanings and connections that group members are drawing from their reading and interaction.

Intention

This multi-step strategy structures exploration and synthesis of information, while incorporating and honoring individual points of view. The physical manipulation and organization of the materials creates a high level of interaction and a visual focusing point for sharing perspectives and clarifying understandings.

Logistics

Materials and Preparation

Blank index cards, 3 per group member

Chart or slide with question prompts for the dialogue

PowerPoint® direction slides

Time

20–30 minutes

Grouping: 4–6

Instructions to Group Leader

1. Direct individuals to read the selected text and use three separate index cards to record: one key word, one phrase, and one sentence. Each card should represent an important idea or concept for that reader.

2. Have group members place their cards by category in the center of the table.

3. Group members then engage in a dialogue to explore the meaning they are making from the text, using the dialogue prompts to structure the conversation.

Tips

The reading can be assigned ahead of the session to maximize the interaction time that group members will have with the text and one another.

Offer the dialogue prompts one at a time to encourage richer exploration of each question.

Variation

Have a different group member facilitate each dialogue prompt. Encourage the facilitator to paraphrase, summarize and organize the thinking of group members and then to probe for clarification and elaboration of ideas.

Example

Dialogue Prompts:

What are some things that pop out for you?

How might you compare and contrast your individual choices?

What are some relationships between the words, phrases and sentences?

What are some connections you are making between this text and your own work?

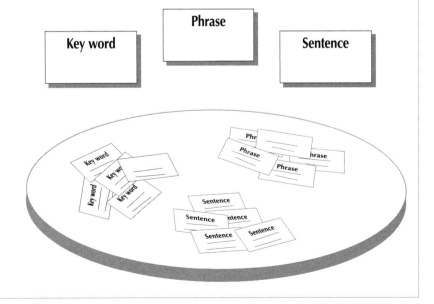

Structuring Group Work

Purposefully structured interactions shape the quality of group members' experience and produce individual and collective learning. These thoughtful design choices influence both group development and task success. Satisfying sessions require an exchange of viewpoints, listening to understand, feelings understood by others and opportunities to influence the final results. Well-engineered work sessions produce these outcomes.

The following elements can be inserted into many of the strategies described in this book. These components can be mixed and matched to amplify the effectiveness of a strategy by shaping interaction or explicit thinking processes.

Interaction Structures

Brainstorm and Pass

Brainstorm and Pass is a structure for balancing participation by having participants brainstorm in sequence. The intention of this structure is to support rapid, non-judgmental generation of ideas.

Directions: One participant begins by offering an idea related to the topic. Additional items are added using a round-robin pattern (see below): one idea at a time, one participant at a time in sequence. To maintain fluidity, group members can "pass," but are still included in subsequent rounds. Note: The recorder also gets a turn in each rotation.

Pairs Squared

Pairs Squared is a structure for expanding a partnered conversation to a larger group in order to extend ideas, connections and perspectives.

Directions: After pairs have been established and completed some aspect of a strategy, invite each pair to join another pair to form quartets. Note: This can be modified to Pairs × Three.

Partner's Report

Partner's Report is a structure for listening to and sharing the ideas of others. This approach produces respectful attention to others' ideas. The structure promotes new voices sharing examples, builds the collective knowledge base and creates fuller community. It's also an opportunity to check for participants' current understanding.

Directions: Individuals generate an idea, recollection, connection, key point, etc. and then share this with a partner. Partners listen to each other and prepare to share their colleague's ideas, not their own. The group leader establishes a sequence or process for sharing with the full group.

Round-Robin

Round-Robin is a structure for balancing participation and providing a space for everyone's contribution by establishing a sequence for sharing.

Directions: Designate a group member to begin sharing. Moving to the right, remaining group members contribute in sequence. Note: One choice point is whether or not each contribution is intended to stimulate conversation or ideas are offered with no cross-talk.

Walk–About

Walk-Abouts provide an opportunity for task groups to view the ideas and work products of others, such as a table or wall chart display. This interaction pattern widens the knowledge base and provides a shift in cognitive and physical energy.

Directions: Establish a time frame and focus for task groups to rotate or move about viewing the work products of other groups. Encourage group members to look for and collect ideas that will stimulate or enhance their own task group work.

Thinking Structures

10-2

10-2, developed by Mary Budd Rowe, is a structure for stimulating attention and retention by providing intermittent breaks for interaction. These brief talk-times occur after approximately ten minutes of input.

Directions: Establish partners and offer a prompt for them to discuss at the point of pause in a presentation. These might include a brief summary, an application, a key point or a question.

From the Balcony

From the Balcony is a structure for shifting perspective to a macro, or bird's eye, view of a situation or event. This view can be applied to past, present or future situations.

Directions: Direct group members to envision or reflect some situation or action, such as an effective lesson, a productive meeting or a parent conference. Have them discuss what they might see and hear from an elevated vantage point. Note: These observations can be organized as a T-Chart.

Stem Completion

Stem Completion is a structure for jumpstarting thoughts and subsequent conversations. This versatile structure can be used before talking with a partner, small group or full group and after group talk to integrate new thinking.

Directions: Offer a visual prompt, on a slide screen, chart or worksheet. Ask individuals to complete the stem. For example, before sharing, ask group members to complete statements such as "One thing I'm looking forward to during this meeting...," or "One thing I noticed about my students this week...." After shared exploration ask group members to complete statements such as "One new idea I will apply...," or "One goal for my own learning...."

Strategies for Forming Groups

Creating purposefully structured task groups fosters relationships and widens perspectives. Periodic regrouping freshens the interactions. This practice is as important for groups of 6 as it is for groups of 60. Static seating produces stale conversations.

The following ideas for grouping are offered to enhance repertoire. They range from very prescribed group compositions to self-selection.

Pre-Established Groups

It is sometimes most effective and time-efficient to determine the group composition before a meeting. For example, a school-wide work session to explore assessment data might benefit from cross-grade or cross-department teams. Consideration for years of teaching experience could be a factor as well. Communicate the groupings ahead of time via email or memo, or on the day of the meeting post charts listing table group assignments for view as people enter the room. Colored dots, symbols or numbers can be added to designate groupings when using nametags.

Grouping During the Meeting

Line-Ups and Count-Offs

Form groups by asking participants to line up, shoulder-to-shoulder, based on a specific criterion, such as length of teaching experience or favorite beverage in alpha order. Once the line is formed, cluster or count-off by the number of desired groups to form the task groups (e.g., a group of 21 people would count-off 1 through 7 to form trios). Count-offs can be used without lining up. Assign participants numbers at their seats then have them join like-numbered colleagues to form new groups.

Using Materials

Cards with shapes or symbols, worksheets with spaces for sign-ups and quotes on colored paper all provide methods for forming groups. For example, a set of cards with colored shapes can be used to form groups with like colors, like shapes or different colors and shapes, depending on the regrouping needs for a session or series of sessions.

Premade worksheets also offer flexibility and can be designed for a specific group. For example, a partnering sheet for a group of science teachers might have four different images of lab equipment with space for a colleague's name beneath each image. Each participant seeks out and signs-up with four different people; making sure names are exchanged and recorded in the corresponding space.

Self-Selection

Preserving participant choice whenever possible is a fundamental principle for working with adults. Toward that end, offer criteria for the expected outcome (e.g., number in group, people not yet worked with, different table) and have groups self-organize based on these factors.

NOTE: Find material masters for several of the grouping strategies described on our website www.miravia.com/groups-at-work.

References

Block, P. 2009. *Community: The Structure of Belonging.* San Francisco: Berrett-Koehler.

DeBono, E. 1992. *Serious Creativity.* New York: Harper Business.

Egawa, K. and Harste, J.C. 2001. "Balancing the Literary Curriculum: A New Vision." *Schooltalk* 7:1–8.

Garmston, R. and Wellman, B. 2013. *The Adaptive School: A Sourcebook for Developing Collaborative Groups,* Second Edition. Lanham, MD: Rowman & Littlefield.

Joyce, B, and Weil, M. 1986. *Models of Teaching.* Englewood Cliffs, NJ: Prentice-Hall.

Kagan, S. 1990. *Cooperative Learning: Resources for Teachers.* Capistrano, CA: Resources for Teachers.

Lipton, L. and Wellman, B. 1998. *Pathways to Understanding: Patterns and Practices in the Learning-Focused Classroom.* Charlotte, VT: MiraVia, LLC.

Saphier, J. and Haley, M. 1993. *Activators: Activity Structures to Engage Student Thinking Before Instruction.* Acton, MA: Research for Better Teaching.

Saphier, J. and Haley, M. 1993. *Summarizers: Activity Structures to Support Integration and Retention of New Learning.* Acton, MA: Research for Better Teaching.

Silberman, M. 1999. *101 Ways to Make Meetings Active.* San Francisco: Jossey-Bass.

Wellman, B. and Lipton, L. 2004. *Data-Driven Dialogue: A Facilitator's Guide to Collaborative Inquiry.* Charlotte, VT: MiraVia, LLC.

Weisbord, M. 2004. *Productive Workplaces: Dignity, Meaning, and Community in the 21st Century.* San Francisco: Jossey-Bass.

Resources

Presentation Skills

Gallo, C. 2010. *The Presentation Secrets of Steve Jobs: How to Be Insanely Great in Front of Any Audience.* New York: McGraw-Hill.

Garmston, R. 2013. *The Presenter's Fieldbook: A Practical Guide,* Second Edition. Lanham, MD: Rowman & Littlefield.

Gottesman, D. and Mauro, B. 2001. *Taking Center Stage: Masterful Public Speaking Using Acting Skills You Never Knew You Had.* New York: Berkeley Books.

Koegel, T. 2007. *The Exceptional Presenter: A Proven Formula to Open Up! and Own the Room.* Austin, TX: Greenleaf Book Group.

Sharp, P. 1993. *Sharing Your Good Ideas: A Workshop Facilitator's Handbook.* Portsmouth, NH: Heinemann.

Taylor, L. 2000. *Stage Performance.* New York: Pocket Books.

Weissman, J. 2009. *Presenting to Win: The Art of Telling Your Story.* Upper Saddle River, NJ: Pearson Education.

Wiskup, M. 2005. *Presentation S.O.S.: From Perspiration to Persuasion in 9 Easy Steps.* New York: Warner Business Books.

Wohlmuth, E. 1983. *The Overnight Guide to Public Speaking.* Philadelphia: Running Press.

Zoller, K. and Landry, C. 2010. *The Choreography of Presenting: The 7 Essential Abilities of Effective Presenters.* Thousand Oaks, CA: Corwin Press.

Presentation Visuals and Projection Timers

Atkinson, C. 2005. *Beyond Bullet Points: Using Microsoft PowerPoint® to Create Presentations That Inform, Motivate, and Inspire.* Redmond, WA: Microsoft Press.

Buckley, M. 2008. *ChartArt Volume 1 and Volume 2.* Charlotte, VT: MiraVia, LLC.

Duarte, N. 2008. Slideology: *The Art and Science of Creating Great Presentations.* North Sebastopol, CA: O'Reilly Media.

Reynolds, G. 2008. *Presentationzen: Simple Ideas on Presentation Design and Delivery.* Berkeley, CA: New Riders.

TimerTools® Software. Timers for digital projection. Supports Windows® and Macintosh® operating systems. http://www.kaganonline.com/catalog/teacher_tools.php#ETT

Facilitating Groups

Bens, I. 2000. *Facilitating with Ease: A Step-by-Step Guidebook.* San Francisco: Jossey-Bass.

Chan, J. 2003. *The Academic Administrator's Guide to Meetings.* San Francisco: Jossey-Bass.

Doyle, M. and Straus, D. 1993. *How to Make Meetings Work: The New Interaction Method.* New York: Berkeley Books.

Glaude, C. 2010. *When Students Fail to Learn: Protocols for a School-Wide Response.* Courtney, BC: Connections Publishing.

Hord, S., Roussin, J., and Sommers, W. 2010. *Guiding Professional Learning Communities: Inspiration, Challenge, Surprise, and Meaning.* Thousand Oaks, CA: Corwin Press.

Kelsey, D. and Plumb, P. 2001. *Great Meetings!: How to Facilitate Like a Pro.* Portland, ME: Hanson Park Press.

McDonald, J., Mohr, N., Dichter, A. and McDonald, E. 2003. *The Power of Protocols: An Educator's Guide to Better Practice.* New York: Teachers College Press.

Schwarz, R. 2002. *The Skilled Facilitator: A Comprehensive Resource for Consultants, Facilitators, Managers, Trainers and Coaches.* San Francisco: Jossey-Bass.

Sibbet, D. 2011. *Visual Meetings: How Graphics, Sticky Notes and Idea Mapping Can Transform Group Productivity.* Hoboken, NJ: John Wiley & Sons.

Straus, D. 2002. *How to Make Collaboration Work: Powerful Ways to Build Consensus, Solve Problems and Make Decisions.* San Francisco: Berrett-Koehler.

Tropman, J. 1996. *Making Meetings Work: Achieving High Quality Group Decisions*. Thousand Oaks, CA: Sage Publications.

Weisbord, M. and Janoff, S. 2007. *Don't Just Do Something, Stand There: Ten Principles for Leading Meetings That Matter*. San Francisco: Berrett-Koehler.

Web Resources

The Center for Graphic Facilitation. Rich links to the world of graphic facilitation including sample graphics, videos, articles and tips as well as links to learning events and resource people. http://graphicfacilitation.blogs. com

Co-Creative Power – A blog on facilitation by Myriam Laberge. A blog the author describes as musings on facilitating effective meetings, public engagement, dialogue and conversations. http://www.myriam-musing. blogspot.com/

ebg consulting – Facilitation resources including a free newsletter, blogs, tips, resources, activities and links to related organizations. http://www. ebgconsulting.com/facres.php

Garr Reynolds website. From the author of *Presentationzen*. A wealth of tips and resources and for creating and making elegant presentations. http://www. garrreynolds.com/

A Graphic Facilitation Retrospective by David Sibbet, the master of this form. http://www.davidsibbet.com/GF%20Retrospective(Updated).pdf

Intro to Graphic Facilitation Tutorials (YouTube Videos). A variety of how-to video clips for aspiring graphic facilitators. http://www.youtube.com/ watch?v=vzfsCtOnERc

Looking at Student Work. This website offers a collection of protocols and tips for helping groups examine student work. http://www.lasw.org/

National School Reform Faculty. A wealth of resources and protocols for group work. http://www.nsrfharmony.org/resources.html

Presentation Magazine. An online resource for information on presentations, speeches and Powerpoint®. http://www.presentationmagazine.com

Roger Schwarz and Associates, Inc. Website of the author of *The Skilled Facilitator*. Sign up here for a free newsletter, browse the article archives and get updates on upcoming training sessions. http://schwarzassociates.com/

Index

About the Authors

Laura Lipton, Ed.D, Co-Director of MiraVia, LLC

Laura Lipton is an instructional strategist who specializes in curriculum and instructional design to promote thinking, learning and thoughtful assessment. Her broad teaching background includes K–12 general and special education and teacher preparation courses. Dr. Lipton has extensive experience in literacy development, curriculum, thinking skills development, thoughtful assessment and Learning-Focused Mentoring. She leads workshops and seminars throughout the United States, Canada, Europe, Australia, Asia and New Zealand.

Contact Laura at:

236 Lucy's Lane, Charlotte, VT 06784
Phone: 802-425-6483 Fax: 802-239-2341 e-mail: lelipton@miravia.com

Bruce Wellman, M.Ed, Co-Director of MiraVia, LLC

Bruce Wellman consults with school systems, professional groups and publishers throughout the United States and Canada, presenting workshops and courses for teachers and administrators on teaching methods and materials, thinking skills development, Learning-Focused Mentoring, presentation skills and facilitating collaborative groups. Mr. Wellman has served as a classroom teacher, curriculum coordinator and staff developer in the Oberlin, Ohio, and Concord, Massachusetts public schools. He holds a B.A. degree from Antioch College and an M.Ed from Lesley College.

Contact Bruce at:

229 Colyer Road, Guilford, VT 05301
Phone: 802.257.4892 Fax: 802.257.2403 e-mail: bwellman@miravia.com